Covering the World

PERSPECTIVES
ON THE NEWS

Other papers in the series:

The New News v. The Old News:
The Press and Politics in the 1990s
Essays by Jay Rosen and Paul Taylor

PERSPECTIVES ON THE NEWS

COVERING THE WORLD

International Television
News Services

Essay by

Lewis A. Friedland

Series Editor: Suzanne Charlé

A Twentieth Century Fund Paper

The Twentieth Century Fund is a research foundation undertaking timely analyses of economic, political, and social issues. Not-for-profit and nonpartisan, the Fund was founded in 1919 and endowed by Edward A. Filene.

Library of Congress Cataloging-in-Publication Data

Friedland, Lewis A.
    Covering the world : international television news services : essay / by Lewis A. Friedland.
        p.   cm. -- (Perspectives on the news ; 2)
    "A Twentieth Century Fund paper."
    Includes bibliographical references and index.
    ISBN 0-87078-345-9 : $8.95
    1. Television broadcasting of news.   I. Twentieth Century Fund.   II. Title.
III. Series.
PN4784.T4F75   1992   92-41333
070.1'95--dc20   CIP

Cover Design and Illustration: Claude Goodwin

Manufactured in the United States of America.

Foreword

From its inception, television's edge in reporting the news was immediacy. Over a single generation, live coverage of news events reshaped political communication, perceptions of the world, and our ideas about shared experience. We saw an alleged presidential assassin killed, a nightly slice of the war in Vietnam, a series of natural and man-made disasters, the opening shots in Baghdad, and embraced televised debates as the climax of political campaigns. We've learned to expect and want the news now.

Overnight delivery, faxes, modems, and computer data bases supply our need for information at a rate that was unthinkable ten, even five, years ago. A part of that demand for instantaneous information has helped bring about the success of international television news. For most people working in the age of information, newspapers just take too long; normal television news presents brief snippets of selected information every so many hours. For the oil trader, the stockbroker, the investment banker, information is money and the best source of information about what is happening in the Middle East, in the free trade talks, in Los Angeles, in useful depth, can be found by switching to CNN.

The pervasiveness of the belief that CNN is where you go to find out "what's really happening" is startling. For the three networks, accustomed to virtually total dominance of television news, the development of CNN couldn't have come at a more awkward time. For the fragmentation of markets accompanying the spread of cable television already has forced a restructuring of network news departments. The big three have closed news bureaus abroad, depending instead on footage provided by newly significant international television news services, World Television News and Visnews. And CNN is where we—and people all over the world—

watched the earthquake's aftermath, watched Hurricane Andrew, watched the Gulf War, watched Tiananmen Square, and saw the wall between the Germanies come down.

One series of questions centers on what all this means for other forms of news. Can the newspapers fight back or will they have to change, hoping to survive by playing a different role, perhaps focusing on local issues? Can network television find a way to compete, increasing its coverage, given the expense of maintaining foreign bureaus, or will it remain increasingly dependent on the same sources for coverage? Another question is what does this mean in terms of the way peoples and nations see the world. Will there emerge a more homogeneous world, a truly global village? And will that village, because of the predominant role of Anglo-American companies in the international television sphere, use our standards of journalism? If it continues to look exclusively Western, will the other nations of the world once again talk of the need for a new international news order?

These questions are complex and vast. The Twentieth Century Fund, which has long had an interest in the media, is examining many of these issues in a series of papers entitled Perspectives on the News. The first volume in the series, *The New News v. The Old News*, published in November, focused on the relationship of press and politics; others in the series will look at such issues as the future of newspapers and privacy and public litigation. This series joins a distinguished list of Twentieth Century Fund publications examining the media, including *The International News Services* by Jonathan Fenby, *Presidential Television* by Newton Minow, Lee Mitchell, and John Bartlow Martin, and *A Free and Balanced Flow: Report of the Task Force on the International Flow of News*.

In this volume, Lewis Friedland, who teaches at the University of Wisconsin-Madison's School of Journalism, has taken a careful look at the issues surrounding the international coverage of world events by networks that have access to the minds of huge numbers of the world's citizens, spanning the globe as it were. He raises questions that we would do well to answer if we are to fill our role as a world leader responsibly. On behalf of the Trustees, I want to thank him for his efforts.

Richard C. Leone, *President*
The Twentieth Century Fund
December 1992

Contents

·1·
The World News Order

T en years ago, there was no international television news network. In the United States, the three major networks—ABC, CBS, and NBC (the Big Three)—fit as much international news into their nightly flagship newscasts as they presumed their audiences needed or wanted to know. They gathered international news from worldwide bureaus concentrated in Western Europe, Tokyo, and Moscow; when they needed video from the Third World, they bought it from the two London-based international television news agencies. Upstart Cable News Network (CNN) was going about the business of establishing a twenty-four-hour cable news network on a shoestring budget, barely noticed by the Big Three.

In Western Europe and Japan, national public service broadcasters were the jewels in the crown of public communication. Gostelradio (GR) was the only broadcasting authority in the then-Soviet Union; in Beijing, the Chinese government television, CCTV, determined nightly news for the People's Republic of China. Much of the Third World was still trying to put demands for a New World Information and Communication Order on the international agenda without much apparent progress. The national broadcasters of many Third World nations depended on the kindness of others for news of the outside world, and the hardware through which it was transmitted. The communications world was divided by the neocolonial lines of the twentieth century, traced on the still-visible spheres of influence of the nineteenth.

In the 1980s, this well-ordered television universe was starting to disintegrate, as pieces of an international television system were being put into place. A series of stories—from the Falklands/Malvinas War in 1982 to the overthrow of Marcos in the Philippines in 1986—began to demonstrate the power of international television to report events in real time. The Reagan-Gorbachev summits reinforced the power of international television to shape public opinion. But it was not until the late 1980s and early 1990s that CNN gained international prominence during a series of crises, including the Tiananmen Square Massacre in China and the Persian Gulf War. CNN pushed the boundaries of world news: No longer did the network merely report events, but through its immediate reportage, CNN actually shaped the events and became part of them. This power not only attracted new viewers to CNN, it also forced American networks to revise their approach to the news. In essence, coverage of the events demonstrated how an international network could function, and stimulated the British Broadcasting Corporation (BBC), Nippon Hoso Kyokai (NHK), and others to consider starting their own international television networks. And it became a laboratory for new uses of news technology.[1]

To better understand just what a sea change this was, let us first look at the coverage of the two incidents.

Tiananmen Square Massacre

By the time of the prodemocracy movement in China in 1989, world television had come of age. Every major country in Europe, Asia, and Africa received CNN, including China and the former Soviet Union. And the world's heads of state and foreign offices had begun using CNN as a medium of diplomatic exchange.

The Beijing Spring—which came to be known as the Tiananmen Square Massacre—was a turning point in the development of the world news system. The most important news story to be covered by international satellite television to that date, it was the first story in which the world television news system directly affected events themselves, while they were occurring, at three specific levels: within national boundaries, throughout the world diplomatic system, and on the stage of international public opinion. It was also a testing ground for comparing CNN's handling of the story with that of its major American network competitors. Finally, coverage of China in 1989 shaped the world news system for years to come: "It was after Tiananmen Square that we really redefined how we do television," according to Susan Zirinsky, a senior producer at CBS. "Berlin Wall falling live on television; bombs over Baghdad, live; scud missiles in Israel, live, live . . . it is a new universe."[2]

The death of proreform Politburo member Hu Yaobang on April 15, 1989, set off the democracy movement on Chinese campuses around

Beijing. In a round of unprecedented bargaining between leaders of the Chinese government, headed by Premier Deng Xiaoping, and student groups, the students raised demands for "democratic reform." This process reached a crisis point with the visit of Soviet president Mikhail Gorbachev on May 15. The international media converging on Beijing for the visit focused a spotlight on the students' demands, which in turn escalated the crisis for the Chinese government, as the occupation of Tiananmen Square continued through Gorbachev's visit. Live satellite transmissions were cut off on May 19, with Gorbachev's departure. The confrontation between the government and students deepened, culminating in the events of June 3–4, the Tiananmen Square Massacre.

The students skillfully used the Western media in several ways. First, they adopted American symbols including "The Goddess of Democracy"; they carried signs with quotations from Abraham Lincoln and Patrick Henry, all in English for the benefit of the Western audience. Although the students were portrayed by American television as having a somewhat naive understanding of these symbols, in fact the student leadership was quite sophisticated. The Beijing students were the future elite of China. Many had been abroad and understood American media. They knew that keeping the cameras on them would be a powerful tool in their struggle, and they also understood that appealing to Americans' traditional belief in the United States as a beacon of democracy would further this goal. In fact, the Big Three all adopted a "prodemocracy" frame for the student movement, despite evidence that the movement's definitions of democracy were extremely broad, and that its stated and actual goals were reform of the Communist system. CNN was a partial exception, using more specific descriptions than its network counterparts. However, according to a study by Harvard's Joan Shorenstein Barone Center, "Turmoil at Tiananmen," ABC, CBS, and CNN all portrayed the story in confrontational terms as a direct student challenge to the Chinese leadership.[3]

The reporting in Beijing also offers a comparison of the various methods of coverage. Typically, the major networks claim to provide depth and perspective that CNN does not, through more experienced anchors, reporters, and producers. CNN counterclaims that the luxury of time allows it to offer fuller treatment of issues. China offers a contrast. Only CNN ran excerpts from official government speeches, press conferences, and CCTV. This coverage reflected CNN's wire-service-like commitment to bring viewers all significant statements from all sides, regardless of whether there were "good pictures." CNN's feature pieces, on the other hand, included descriptions of biking in Beijing and a montage of natural street sounds intercutting traditional dragon dancing and dragon images. In contrast, at the beginning of Gorbachev's visit on May 15, CBS's Bruce Morton filed a background piece in which he effectively portrayed the poverty of student lives as one major element in their political frustration. For CNN, perspective resided in the breadth of its coverage, and the commitment that all significant stories and points of view would be aired. For CBS, perspective came from the background it provided.

The China story also marked the first time a major breaking story was covered twenty-four hours a day for a worldwide television audience. This meant, in essence, that traditional deadlines were telescoped. Until China, the traditional print wire services had the relative luxury of holding a story until it could be checked out to editors' satisfaction. With the presence of CNN, the wire services had live competition. Because government-run news agencies are widely understood by the Chinese people to be political conduits, news in the streets travels by rumor. Rumor is easily manipulated by political factions, and the students understood that, as significant sources for reporters, they could sometimes get unconfirmed stories aired that would reflect very unfavorably on the government. Before the night of June 3, waves of rumors swept Beijing concerning impending troop movements on Tiananmen Square, and the fall of either Zhao Ziyang or Deng Xiaoping. When CNN was forced to decide whether to report these rumors or not, it chose to do so. CNN International editor Eason Jordan said: "We know we're on the air twenty-four hours a day. But we don't put information on the air that might be construed as irresponsible. . . . [CNN correspondent Mike] Chinoy was reporting information from sources, some of which some people might say was rumor. When rumor is that big a part of the story, you just have to say so. But we never billed rumor as fact."[4]

What CNN reported became more significant because it was a primary source for other news organizations. Editors at the *Washington Post* and Associated Press used CNN as a video wire throughout the crisis. Some reporters, especially from the wire services, complained that their editors would see reports on CNN and then send them out to check on stories that the reporters in the field thought were unlikely. Others, like UPI's David Schweisberg, said that CNN was "more right than wrong." CNN's Vito Maggioli, then a producer in China, explained the problem this way: "There is this twenty-four-hour machine. . . . You have to constantly be thinking about what do we have here, what are we going to do with it, can we wait, should we wait?"[5]

CNN's coverage often set the news agenda for other news organizations. Any reported rumors had to be checked out, and sometimes those rumors gained political and diplomatic force that reverberated long after they were disproved. On June 5, for instance, immediately after the massacre, a "U.S. intelligence" estimate of the death toll was widely reported as 3,000; the background source was Secretary of State James Baker. Four U.S. government sources anonymously told the writers of the Harvard study that the 3,000 figure was an extrapolation of the 2,600 figure released by the Chinese Red Cross and reported by CNN and ABC. The figures were later revised downward to between 400 and 800.

The coverage had a clear effect both within and outside of China. For the Chinese people themselves, radio was much more important than television. Both the Voice of America (VOA) and BBC World Service were readily available, and VOA broadcasts were regularly translated into posters and placed on walls. Although CNN had achieved the most significant television presence in Beijing, it was mostly accessible in hotels with an overwhelmingly foreign audience. However, according to Mark Hopkins, VOA's Beijing bureau chief, hundreds of young English-speaking Chinese staff did watch CNN in the hotels.[6] There is anecdotal evidence that word of CNN's telecasts also got out into the streets. According to CNN's Alec Miran, who was executive producer in China at the time, "People were coming up to us in the street, telling us to 'Keep going, keep broadcasting, that they won't come in while you're on the air.' That turned out to be true. The troops went in after our cameras were shut down."[7]

New technology was thrown into the breach during the China story, and old technology was used in new and innovative ways. While satellite news gathering was not new, CNN pioneered the use of "fly-away packs," portable satellite news-gathering gear that could be packed in a number of crates and set up at virtually any site. CNN also used cellular telephones to feed voice reports, "phoners," from Tiananmen Square to Atlanta. CNN had ordered the cellular connections before the crackdown, and they were left in place. (CNN remembered its use of telephone lines in Beijing when planning for Baghdad; perhaps the Big Three did not.) On June 12, after the crackdown, CNN also flew in "handicams," miniature 8mm video cameras, after it was no longer safe to use regular-sized field gear. Handicams were used surreptitiously by CNN crews riding bicycles around Beijing to get footage. This was not a case of a new technology being available to CNN. Rather, perhaps because of its unorthodox operating methods, CNN was willing to use the smaller cameras—often scorned as "toys"—on a breaking story.

The Chinese government clearly grasped the link between satellite transmission and its world standing. Both CBS and CNN had obtained permission to operate their satellite uplinks only during the week of Gorbachev's visit. CNN brought in its own portable satellite fly-away dish; both CBS and CNN transmitted their pictures from Tiananmen Square via cable to CCTV, and from there back to their hotels. Two sep-arate, dramatic confrontations occurred, the first between Dan Rather and CCTV officials, the second between CNN's Alec Miran and government officials. The shutdown of live transmissions visually personified gov-ernment repression for American and world audiences. Shortly after the satellite shutdowns, the U.S. government issued a formal protest— via CNN—about what President Bush had just witnessed in China while watching CNN from his summer home in Kennebunkport, Maine.

The traditional relation between U.S. public opinion and diploma-cy was inverted during the Tiananmen Square Massacre. While the cri-sis unfolded on television, U.S. policymakers were forced to take what the nation's people were seeing into account *while* creating policy. The tension of the crisis was heightened, shortening the time for acceptable diplomatic response. When American viewers could see troops moving into Tiananmen Square, it became impossible for the Bush administra-tion to avoid a public condemnation of the Chinese government, how-ever much it may have wished to do so, and despite its conviction that quiet diplomacy would have been more effective. According to *Time*, State Department spokesperson Margaret Tutweiler dragged Secretary of State Baker to watch CNN's coverage of the Tiananmen crackdown. Moreover, *Time* quotes a "senior official" on CNN's coverage: "It demand-ed a solution we couldn't provide. We were powerless to make it stop."[8]

Indeed, CNN became the primary source of information for much of the U.S. government. According to one Capitol Hill staff member, "The *[New York] Times* and the evening newscasts were a day late . . . [and] there was not much time to read or watch media. It was CNN that deter-mined the base of events, throughout the beltway. The images of that night were the primary stimulus for the feeding frenzy that took place here in Congress immediately afterward."[9]

CNN's presence in Beijing intensified the interaction between the American public and the American government; that call and response would likely have been there had only CBS been present. But CNN was viewed worldwide, at least by elite audiences. The Chinese government knew precisely what U.S. leaders were seeing and the kind of pressure it would place on them. Likewise, U.S. officials knew that the same events were being seen in London, Paris, Tokyo, and Moscow, and this also pres-sured them to act on a newly emerging stage of world diplomatic opin-ion. The events in China did not attain the full wiring of the diplomatic circuit that would occur during the Persian Gulf War, but they did forcefully demonstrate that world events could no longer be restricted to exchanges among one or several nations at a pace dictated solely by the leadership of the superpowers.

The War in the Persian Gulf

If the China crisis established CNN and world television as a legitimate force, the Gulf War placed CNN in the forefront of the broadcast world and increased the pressure on other players to enter the global news competition.[10]

The Gulf War demonstrated the strengths of international television as a medium of diplomacy and as a witness to events. At the same time, it demonstrated how world television could be bent to follow lines favorable to the dominant Western nations that were the base of that system.

CNN's function as a diplomatic news wire was well established by the time of Iraqi president Saddam Hussein's invasion of Kuwait in August 1990. Speaking at a Stanford University symposium on global communication in 1990, George Shultz, former secretary of state, described how the officer at the State Department operations desk always had a television tuned to CNN. While this did not seem unusual, Shultz said he was surprised that when he visited the foreign ministries of other nations, their operations officers were also watching CNN.[11] During the events leading up to the war, CNN operated as a diplomatic seismograph. Immediately after the August 1990 invasion of Kuwait, President Bush publicly referred to CNN on several occasions. Tariq Aziz, Iraqi foreign minister, made reference to President Bush's news conferences televised on CNN; during subsequent formal diplomatic exchanges, Kuwait's foreign minister referred to comments that reflected Aziz's prior CNN comments. The use of CNN as a diplomatic party line became almost comical at times. During the Gulf buildup, President Turgut Ozal of Turkey was watching a CNN telecast of a news conference given by President Bush. He heard a reporter ask Bush whether Ozal would cut off Turkey's oil pipeline into Iraq. Bush said he was about to ask Ozal the same question. When Ozal's telephone rang, he told Bush he was expecting the call. As Richard Haass, National Security Council aide to President Bush, told *Time*: "You end up hearing statements for the first time, not in diplomatic notes, but because you see a foreign minister on the screen. By television, I really mean CNN. It has turned out to be a very important information source."[12]

As the crisis moved closer to war, CNN became an unofficial line of communication within the U.S. government. President Bush reportedly told other world leaders, "I learn more from CNN than I do from the CIA." After the start of the air war, Secretary of Defense Richard Cheney said at a press conference, "The best reporting I saw on what transpired in Baghdad was on CNN." In *The Commanders*, Bob Woodward recounts the regular monitoring of CNN in the period leading up to the war. After the air war was launched, in secret, Cheney went back to his office and turned on CNN. "He thought the first leak or hint that the air operation was underway would most likely come from the twenty-four-hour news service." When CIA Director William Webster received word that an Iraqi missile had been launched, he reportedly told National Security Council Adviser Brent Scowcroft "turn on CNN to see where it lands." Indeed, in place of the standard "no comment," State Department, Pentagon, and military spokespersons would regularly respond to questions with "I don't know anymore than what you saw on CNN."[13]

This was, of course, not true. There was information available to government officials of which the public was never informed, and the standard CNN disclaimer served as a convenient excuse for nondisclosure, a part of the government's propaganda war. What was remarkable, however, was the extent to which government officials *did* appear to rely on CNN as their primary source of breaking news.

During the Gulf crisis, both sides saw CNN as part of an international battleground for public opinion. Beyond its role in diplomacy, CNN was the staging ground for massive public opinion campaigns. President Sadaam Hussein of Iraq used CNN several times. Shortly after the invasion of Kuwait, he seized a group of predominantly American and British hostages and moved them to military installations as "human shields." As Western public opinion turned against Sadaam Hussein, he went on Iraqi television to "visit" with the British hostages. The meeting was carried around the world by CNN. Clearly Sadaam Hussein believed his "visit" was an effective propaganda move; CNN was widely condemned for airing the meeting. Nevertheless, the staged quality of the meeting, and its international distribution, only served to discredit Sadaam as a clumsy propagandist. At the end of January, after the start of the air war, Hussein again appealed to international public opinion in an exclusive interview with CNN's Peter Arnett, the only Western correspondent then operating out of Baghdad. Hussein threatened to use chemical warheads and expressed regret at letting his hostages go. Arnett sent out the interview via a flyaway satellite uplink, with the single comment: "Chilling."

Arnett's reporting from Baghdad was attacked by the Bush administration and its supporters as "Iraqi propaganda." However, the U.S. military also used CNN to its advantage in the public opinion war. The daily U.S. military briefings, televised in full as they occurred on CNN, were staged news events. American military public affairs officers and briefers skillfully used the briefings to convey sanitary images of the war to the American people—for example, the smart bomb videos—and sometimes to send messages to the Iraqis. When transports of the 82nd Airborne Division arrived in Saudi Arabia in August 1990, General Norman Schwartzkopf made sure they were covered by television, because he knew Sadaam Hussein was watching CNN. In February, after Iraqi command and control was presumably shattered by U.S. bombing, a high-ranking U.S. intelligence officer said of Hussein: "CNN may have been the only accurate source of information that he had. So we knew what he was getting. We were able to pass information to him."[14]

CNN, as is widely known, was the only network to send news out of Baghdad on January 16, 1991, the night U.S. air attacks were launched. CNN obtained permission from the Iraqi government to place an uninterruptable "four-wire" telephone hookup in Baghdad. The result was the riveting Shaw-Holliman-Arnett reporting during the air attacks. ABC, CBS, and NBC news staffers groused (without evidence) that CNN had to do special favors for the Iraqi government, some implying that bribes were paid. CNN executives say they simply planned better, worked harder, and were more persistent. Stuart Loory, a former newspaperman and now a CNN vice president, points to CNN's ongoing relation with Iraqi television: "When Iraq's invasion of Kuwait took place, we were probably the only American network that had good contacts with Iraqi television. The year before, we had the director general of Iraqi television right here in Atlanta at a 'World Report' contributors conference. We had spent hours trying to arrange Iraq's contributions for the 'World Report,' going back probably three years before that happened."[15] The Big Three's complaints paled alongside CNN's obvious scoop, and the night of January 16 has since entered journalism lore.

The networks and some critics complained further that CNN was a loose cannon, diluting traditional network depth and perspective, airing unsubstantiated live reports. When Tom Shales of the *Washington Post* criticized CNN's live reporting, saying "liveliness is not next to godliness" and that "CNN pulled some tremendous scoops, but also lots of blunders," he was widely understood to have been reflecting the viewpoint of network insiders, especially at CBS. Shales contrasted his criticism of CNN with praise of network professionalism.

The criticism that CNN lacks depth angers CNN executive producer Robert Furnad. "First of all they can't outdo our analysis when they are doing a half an hour a day and we are doing eighteen hours a day. Where we have been weaker is in compiling at the end of the day, the packaging, but we have made great gains." Furnad says that it is absurd to say "when CNN offers an eight-minute interview and the networks a fifteen-second clip that the nets have greater depth and analysis." He in turn criticizes the networks: "What amazes me about the networks and all the creative geniuses is that they don't know how to do live television."[16]

During the Gulf War, CNN's perspective showed up in places other than the anchor desk. One was the regular appearance of foreign journalists on CNN, the only unfiltered, non-American viewpoints, and certainly the only unmediated views from the Arab world, to appear regularly on American television. The two regular fora were "World Report" and "International Correspondents," a roundtable discussion of journalists from countries other than the United States. "World Report" offered the only uncensored world public opinion on the war accessible to the American public in a significant viewing time slot. "World Report" included stories from U.S. allies, opponents, and Third World nations, many of which were critical of the United States' conduct of the war. "World Report" executive producer Donna Mastrangelo noted, "Iran contributes to 'World Report' regularly, Saudi Arabia does, Kuwait does, they all do in the Gulf region. . . . Getting reports helped form a different perspective."[17] "International Correspondents" featured regular discussions with world journalists. The most striking programs featured Arab journalists from Egypt, Lebanon, Jordan, and Syria, as well as Palestinians. By presenting the unmediated views of journalists who were not recognized as experts by the three networks and PBS, "International Correspondents" presented the most openly critical discussion of America's actions in the war from an Arab point of view to a mass American audience.[18]

Another innovation during the war was introduced on the "Larry King" show, a talk radio show brought to television: an international call-in line. This turned the King show into the first international call-in show on television. The King show functioned as a kind of nightly town-hall meeting of the air, in sharp contrast with CBS's "America Tonight" with Charles Kuralt and Leslie Stahl. CBS launched the program during the Gulf War, perhaps hoping for a repeat of "Nightline's" success a decade earlier. "America Tonight" consciously developed the image of a folksy town meeting, reflected in a patriotic format and the choice of Kuralt. In actual content, however, the program relied on the same narrow range of experts as other network programs.

By the traditional standards of the television news battles, CNN demonstrated during the early days of the war that it could "out-cover" the Big Three, even though CBS and ABC eventually caught up (NBC never did).

And ABC and CBS brought some perspective through their anchors and field correspondents that CNN did not have. However, CNN remained the first source for news. For all practical purposes it became the newswire for other news organizations. CBS analyst retired general Michael Dugan said of his work for CBS during the war: "What CBS did during the Gulf War was watch CNN." And *New York Times* foreign editor Bernard Gwertzman commented, "Like everyone else, we're thankful for CNN. It's become the unpaid news service for papers. We rely on it an enormous amount."[19]

CNN's success and influence during the Tiananmen Square Massacre, the Gulf War, and the attempted Soviet coup (which shall be considered later) has established it as the preeminant global television news service. Today, CNN International (CNNI) reaches a global audience of fifty-three million viewers in 138 nations; in the United States, CNN reaches about sixty million households. As a twenty-four-hour service, it has changed the way television can be used. At any given moment less than 1 percent of the American viewing audience is watching CNN. During any week, however, about 25 percent of the viewers will have checked in with CNN. In contrast, viewers watch the Big Three nightly newscasts in numbers ranging from 11 to 15 percent every night. The networks provide the day's headlines in twenty-two minutes. CNN is there twenty-four hours a day, to be taken as needed. Robert Ross, Turner Broadcasting System's vice president for international business development, says: "I think people buy CNN not because they want to watch it at this particular point in time, but they buy it for the option to watch it when they want to, which is to say when something important happens which is worth watching. And this is how you explain that CNN has such low ratings, and yet so many people have bought it."[20]

It is precisely this twenty-four-hour option that distinguishes CNN from its domestic and international competitors. CNN is now capable of feeding news from virtually any point on the globe to Atlanta, and from there sending it back out to any point on the globe. This point-to-point structure is the hallmark of the emerging international television system.

CNN, however, is not the only global news service. In recent years other services have started up, in part because other nations do not want to rely on what they see as news with a distinctly American bias, and in part because they see a new market opening. The most prominent is the renowned British Broadcasting Company (BBC), which launched its World Service Television (WSTV) in 1991. Although it is strongest in Asia and Europe, WSTV is establishing a presence in Africa and Canada and is actively searching for partners elsewhere. BBC executives promise that the legacy of BBC World Service Radio will make up for lost time and opportunity. Japan's NHK flirted with the idea of launching Global News Network during 1991 but has since retreated, leaving the international field to CNN and the BBC, at least for the time being.

If CNN and WSTV are the only *global* networks, a second tier is growing below them, continent by continent and nation by nation. Broadcasters in the European Community, also hesitant at being dependent on the United States for their news, have launched Euronews, an all-news satellite channel set to begin broadcasting in five languages in 1993. In addition to this, Rupert Murdoch's Sky News, headquartered in Britain, has launched a private news channel for Europe, and the new Middle East Broadcasting Center (MBC) has been launched, in Arabic, also from London. Televisa of Mexico covers Latin America with its Spanish language service. And the BBC is already being delivered to most of Asia via its partner Star TV, with Cantonese and Mandarin available on second audio channels.

The influence of this patchwork global system is growing rapidly, reshaping our conceptions of politics, culture, and collective identity. It has become a seismograph—a monitoring system for diplomats, financial traders and institutions, and other news organizations— instantly flashing images around the world that nations may once have been able to suppress. It gathers, interprets, transmits, and feeds back information in a continuous loop, changing the course of events in the process of reporting on them. But before we can examine what this system is and what it will mean to our reporting and understanding of world news in the future, we must first go back to the beginnings of satellite television.

•2•
Satellite Television and CNN

The launch of RCA's Satcom I satellite in 1975 brought twenty-four-hour cable programming to the continental United States. Time Inc. leased a transponder for satellite delivery of Home Box Office (HBO), its fledgling movie channel, which became the fastest-growing cable service in the late 1970s. Atlanta television entrepreneur Ted Turner was not far behind: Recognizing the potential value of this satellite real estate, he ordered options on two of the transponders of Satcom I. The first was for his small, Atlanta-based UHF television station, WTCG, which went up on "the bird" in 1976 and was renamed SuperStation WTBS in 1980. TBS stood for Turner Broadcasting System; at the time it seemed a bit grandiose for a station that had been delivering old movies, sitcoms, and losing sports teams across the South. Turner asked RCA about leasing the other transponder for the first all-news channel on television.[21]

WTBS succeeded because it came from the South and went out to rural America, to the many places that had no independent television stations. WTBS became the independent for "the rest of America," and this set the tone for how America received Turner and his network. For those outside the urban orbit, it was the little network that could. For bicoastal network executives, it was a hayseed network, if they noticed it at all.

Hayseed or not, by 1978 Turner's SuperStation WTBS was established as one of the twelve channels that most cable systems carried. The success of WTBS offered a warning, one the major networks universally ignored. Turner saw that the cable industry would need more programming, and his thoughts turned back to news. He called Reese Schonfeld of the Independent Television News Association (ITNA), a television news cooperative of independent stations, to ask how a twenty-four-hour news service could be put together. Schonfeld laid out the groundwork for what would become CNN and eventually CNNI.

As Schonfeld outlined it, the network news venture would require an electronic newsroom, tied together by computers and video editing machines. The new network must be nonunion. It would function as a news cooperative, developing exchange agreements with local stations to reduce the costs of news gathering in the field, and simultaneously gaining wide access to the entire United States. The same cost-driven strategy would apply at an international level. To attain a global reach, the network would exchange news video with other nations via satellite. By pursuing these exchange agreements, the network could keep bureau staff to a minimum. The newswire concept would also emphasize live programming. The network would go live as much as possible, in part to fill time and keep costs low. Schonfeld estimated the initial costs at $15 million to $20 million, with operating costs of about $2 million a month. This was at a time when the Big Three were spending $100 million to $150 million a year on news.[22]

Turner's original vision for CNN's format was inspired by the Time-Life magazine empire. CNN was to have news like *Time*, sports like *Sports Illustrated*, soft features like *People*, and business news like *Fortune*. This material would be organized into a "newswheel," an idea borrowed from Westinghouse-owned WINS radio in New York City, which built its reputation on the slogan: "Give us twenty-two minutes; we'll give you the world." Live news would be the new network's signature. Hard news stories would revolve every hour, being updated as needed. These stories would be blended with weather, sports, and softer features, all of which could be trimmed, dropped, or reshuffled when live news broke. With the revolving format and regular cut-ins of live reports, CNN would be able to fill its twenty-four hours.

Several format concepts born of necessity later became CNN hallmarks. All were rooted in the new network's economics. It was clear from the outset that if Turner was going to spend $25 million to $30 million a year to do twenty-four hours of news a day, then the existing financial structure of the networks would have to be turned upside down, starting with work rules and labor structure.

CNN would not be able to hire the sophisticated behind-the-scenes talent of ABC, CBS, and NBC. Each network employed a large headquarters staff in New York, with a series of managing editors, assignment desk people, and assistants. New York supervised bureaus around the nation and the world, each of which had parallel chains of command. Producers gathered, processed, and packaged the news, working with correspondents whose stories often had long lead times.

Network unionization not only raised salaries up and down the chain of command, but—to CNN's way of thinking—unions sustained complicated and outmoded work rules. CNN could not afford to replicate this system and survive as a twenty-four-hour service.

As CNN raced to get on the air by June 1, 1980, it was forced to build an entirely new computerized news operation and then "hire a network," all within six months' time. A team of computer programmers created the BASYS system, which would soon become the standard throughout the television industry. This system integrated newswires, the assignment desk, producers, graphics rundowns, tape lists, and anchor scripts. Driven by cost, CNN created the first newsroom completely integrated by computers, an "electronic newsroom."

Changing the network labor structure was more difficult. CNN executives had to decide which job categories must be filled from within the existing television labor pool, and from what levels. Frontline anchors and producers needed to be experienced, yet because the pay for even secondary network talent ranged from $60,000 up to $1 million plus, only a few could come from the three major networks. CNN hired former CBS News star Daniel Schorr as a commentator; anchor Bernard Shaw and Washington bureau chief George Watson came from ABC. But the rest of the anchor talent pool came from outside the major television markets, places like Salt Lake City and New Orleans, where talent was paid $30,000 to $60,000, well under even the lowest network salaries. Because it could not afford big-name national anchor talent, CNN had no choice but to "put the news first."

Even this midmarket talent was relatively expensive. Bureau chiefs and a few producers could come from the networks and medium-large markets. To fill the gap below these levels—the ranks of assistant producers and rewrite people, assignment desk assistants, videotape editors, and assistant directors—the network came up with the idea of "video journalists": young people just out of college, working long hours with no fixed work rules for little money. The so-called VJs wrote, produced, edited tape, ran cameras, and operated control-room equipment. This strategy required total flexibility. VJs could produce in the morning, edit tape in the afternoon, and run camera at night, without ever becoming producer, editor, or camera operator. In this one massive stroke, CNN destroyed fifty accumulated years of network work rules. VJs were paid just above minimum wage, apprentices to a system they were helping to invent as they went along.

Putting a pool of inexperienced talent at the core of such a complicated system, which was dedicated to airing as much live television as possible, inevitably meant on-air glitches and gaffes that would have been intolerable even at medium-sized network affiliates. The necessity of reducing costs pushed CNN to redefine how television should look. The familiar grammar of television—the calm, controlled anchor-in-charge flawlessly handing off to correspondents who then presented perfectly edited packages—was the network standard, emulated if not always achieved at most network affiliates and independents alike. CNN would necessarily be ragged, and so it made raggedness a virtue. The live, "you are there" quality of CNN was built in from the beginning (even when there wasn't much live action to see).

Perhaps the most significant long-term innovation was the way that CNN put together its domestic and international video news-gathering operations. Schonfeld's experience at ITNA had demonstrated the possibilities of using affiliates as primary news-gathering sources for a network. CNN would be built this way from the ground up. The domestic desk was established through reciprocal agreements with local news organizations, one at a time. The idea was simple. CNN offered its service via satellite to hundreds of stations throughout the United States in exchange for their video. By giving away its own product, CNN rapidly built up an affiliate network that, in breadth, rivaled that of the Big Three.[23] By 1982, CNN had reciprocity agreements with about 125 local broadcasters. In years to come, CNN and its "affiliates" would begin to cut out the middlemen, the network news operations, on breaking stories.

The same principle was applied to international affiliates. CNN's foreign editor approached both public and commercial networks of other nations to exchange video on a story-by-story basis. Virtually none of the broadcasters outside of the United States had ever heard of CNN. But as these relationships were built over CNN's first years, an international network of affiliates gradually fell into place. Again, necessity became a virtue. While the Big Three disdained the idea of using the video of other news services and relied on the international news agencies only when they could not produce video out of their own bureaus, CNN could not afford this luxury. CNN was building the first international television news cooperative brick by brick.

Perhaps most important, CNN was committed to going live with breaking stories as often as possible. CNN was predisposed to live television for two reasons. Most of its news managers, on-air talent, and producers were products of local stations and had come of age with local television in the 1970s, the heyday of live local "action" news. While networks rarely went live, even during major stories, local news was often live every night, whether a story required it or not. Local news managers understood the excitement that could be generated by "bringing the viewer there." Stuart Loory calls this the "live philosophy": "We used to talk about it a lot in the early years—the idea that we practice kind of a raw journalism in which we take our viewers with us to the scene of the story," he said. "And we give them the opportunity to be the journalists along with us. And that is to assimilate the information and make up their own minds about just what it is they're seeing or hearing."[24] Live television immediately distinguished CNN from the Big Three, whose executives ridiculed CNN's live propensities, at least for a while.

The second reason was economic. Once CNN had paid for satellite time, the blocks might as well be filled with live television. It gave viewers new stories, or new angles on breaking stories, and it slowed down the merciless newswheel. Live programming could also be less expensive to produce. The live philosophy became a distinguishing mark of CNN in its early years, although the strategy caused the fledgling network some embarrassments. Ten weeks after CNN went on the air, its anchors were covering the 1980 Democratic National Convention. However, due to a lack of funds, there were no walls in the skybooth and everytime the band struck up, it drowned out CNN's anchors. Things soon improved, and by 1981 CNN scooped the Big Three on the attempted assassination of President Reagan. The early glitches turned out to have been dress rehearsals for a new kind of television.

CNN had the tone of a local news operation, even when it was covering national and international stories, and this was part of its middle-American appeal. Lacking the sophistication of the Big Three's anchors and correspondents, CNN's on-air talent were more like the local news stars from whom viewers heard tales of tornadoes, crime, and local corruption. Essentially, they were more "approachable," not a quality normally attributed to network news anchors. CNN video was more ragged and uneven, like the local news sources and stringers from which it often came. The "live" commitment of the network also made it seem more like local television. Far from being something to hide, this was appealing to CNN's viewers; the U.S. news market was changing rapidly, a fact that seemed to pass by the Big Three.

The Changing Network News Business

As CNN prepared to go on the air in 1980, the Big Three continued with business as usual. HBO had been showing some success since 1975, but pay television was only a rivulet in the revenue stream. Twenty percent of American homes owned VCRs, remote controls had begun to appear, and cable reached 19 percent of homes with televisions; nonetheless, the Big Three still attracted nine out of ten American viewers every night.[25]

When CNN first appeared, network comment ranged from skeptical to caustic. In 1980, CBS News vice president Burton Benjamin spoke for many of his colleagues when he told the *New York Times*, "I don't think people want to just watch some guy rip and read the news off the wires, but once you start moving crews into hot spots, the money's heavy. On a big story, say in Cuba or Iran, you might have to send two or three crews. One trip like that and you could feed a family of four for a year." ABC News president Roone Arledge added, "I like the idea of an all-news network, but we run through the thirty million dollars they're talking about spending for a year in two or three months."[26]

By 1986, the comments would be reversed. Capital Cities took over ABC in January. General Electric acquired NBC along with parent company RCA in June. Laurence Tisch of Loews swallowed CBS in September while acting as William Paley's "white knight" to defend a network weakened from a hostile takeover by, of all people, Ted Turner. Each of the new owners wanted to know: Why is CNN producing six times as much news at a third of the cost and making $40 million (in 1986) to boot?[27] Far from being a bargain-basement version of the Big Three news divisions, CNN began to represent the vision of their future.

There were now two priorities at the network news divisions: first, to cut costs, and second, to expand audience. At the height of their influence, the networks had been willing to let the news divisions lose money because they were viewed as prestigious and demonstrated to the Federal Communications Commission that the networks operated in the public interest. By the late 1980s, those halcyon days were over. The deregulatory trend that had begun in the mid-1970s was accelerated by the Reagan administration. Television news had been a local profit center at least since the early 1970s. The networks began to expect their own news programs to follow suit. This shift had been under way for some time. The broadcast magazine "60 Minutes" had long demonstrated that crossover programming produced by the news division—news shows with entertainment value— could make a great deal of money that would go straight into network coffers, which wasn't the case for popular programming bought from Hollywood. During the 1980s, however, entertainment values moved from the periphery of the news operation—the morning and late-night shows, the news magazines—into the heart of the network evening news broadcasts. In the old system, money was made and entertainment values tolerated elsewhere to protect the power and integrity of the worldwide news organizations and the nightly newscasts. Now the flagships were no longer protected from either the budget ax or entertainment values.

The cutbacks have had clear consequences for international coverage. International bureaus have been slashed at all three networks. By 1991, ABC had closed its bureaus in Hong Kong, Rome, and Frankfurt, leaving an international total of nine; CBS was left with seven, and NBC ten permanent and several temporary bureaus. (On the domestic side, all three had closed or consolidated bureaus in major U.S. cities including Chicago, Dallas, and Boston.) In 1992, the three networks covered less foreign news than in any of the previous three years, and that wasn't just because of the presidential election. CBS's Dan Rather told the *New York Times*, "We do fewer long pieces about foreign news than we did seven, eight years ago. That's true for all three networks." The trend is clear. If the networks close bureaus in Boston, they surely won't keep them in Bangkok. The cutback in bureaus is only the confirmation of a fundamental shift in the networks' mission. When the press plane covering President Bush was grounded in April 1991 because of a lack of network interest, "NBC Nightly News" executive producer Steve Friedman summed it up this way: "We're doing this to save money, yes, but our role is changing, too. We're not in the overall killer-coverage business anymore. We're in the program business."[28]

If the networks are not in the killer-coverage business, then they do not need to cover breaking events around the world. It's enough to have *pictures* of breaking events, which can be packaged for their programs. This has led to a scramble for joint ventures or ownership stakes in the two major television news picture agencies, Visnews and World Television News (WTN), which between them have broadcast customers in eighty-four countries. ABC holds 80 percent ownership in WTN, the remainder divided between Britain's ITN and Channel 9 Australia. In July 1992, the British news agency Reuters took full control of Visnews from its partners, NBC and the BBC. The agreement gave NBC the right to sell its news pictures worldwide, but left Reuters in control of the world's largest television picture agency. At the time of the buyback, NBC and Reuters made a general announcement of a "joint interest" in international ventures, with suggestions of future cooperation, but no specific plans have been announced. CBS has switched to Visnews as its main supplier of international pictures, but it remains the only network without a long-term relationship with an agency.[29] Rupert Murdoch's Fox News is a Visnews client, while CNN has a long-standing relationship with WTN.

The reasons for the reliance on the agencies are obvious. "It's phenomenally less expensive compared to doing it yourself," says Paul Amos, executive vice president of Fox News, a start-up organization that Murdoch hopes to combine with his British SkyNews. Bureaus cost a bare minimum of $250,000 a year, with additional satellite costs ranging from tens to hundreds of thousands of dollars, depending on location and use. Because bureaus have traditionally covered regions and even continents, costs multiply for each story covered by bureaus in the field. When these same stories can be covered by local or regional crews working for the news agencies, often stringers, the savings are enormous. All three networks are now actively pursuing bureau sharing, according to Joseph Peyronnin, a vice president of CBS News: "Having lots of big bureaus dotted around the world isn't necessary in the 1990's." Peyronnin told the *New York Times* that a more cost-effective strategy is to have a few bureaus in key places and that more cross-border broadcaster-to-broadcaster ventures may be the wave of the future. NBC now shares bureaus in Moscow and Johannesburg with Visnews, and this type of arrangement is likely to expand. According to NBC senior vice president Jay Fine, "It doesn't make sense for five crews to show up and shoot the same pictures of a plane crash. That's not what distinguishes one network from the others. It's the writing, how you put it all together."[30]

This network rationale for the closing of bureaus and the "downsizing" of worldwide coverage reflects a long-standing problem in the coverage of international news for an American audience. Plane crashes highlighting American victims, disasters, wars, and coups have long been the stock in trade of the major networks' international coverage. Network coverage of other nations has always tended toward the type of spectacular and episodic events that make good pictures. Coverage of ongoing international issues and problems that don't offer visuals—agriculture and world hunger, development, health, infant mortality—have been given short shrift.[31] This kind of coverage is not likely to increase with the closing of bureaus and increased dependence on the television agencies for pictures. Despite network protest to the contrary, there was precious little depth in international news coverage before the cutbacks; it's unrealistic to think that perspective will blossom now.

At the height of American influence in the 1960s, the Big Three did export much of their news material, primarily to Europe and Japan. Still, their worldwide system of bureaus reflected a more narrow mission of packaging the news for American audiences. This American perspective was affordable as long as the post-World War II television oligopoly held together. The networks were importers and packagers of foreign events for domestic consumption, not—primarily—exporters of U.S. news to the rest of the world. The international sales of network news departments were secondary, a way to offset the costs of the extensive system of worldwide bureaus.[32] In the new era of corporate ownership, there is economic incentive to water down the product, especially if, as assumed, the customers, the American public, don't care or won't notice the difference.

This is not to say the networks have no international ambitions. When General Electric took over NBC, new president Robert Wright looked toward Europe. GE was a multinational financial company, with a concentrated interest in technology, but it had no experience in broadcasting. While Wright and his GE mentor, Jack Welch, understood the need to position GE globally as a communications conglomerate, they weren't quite sure how to go about it. News might be a part of this mix, but only if it paid its own way.

Wright had a fascination with CNN. According to former NBC News president Reuven Frank, "When Bob Wright took over NBC, we overlapped for about six months, and all he could talk about was CNN. There was a big bank robbery out in Burbank, and KNBC put five or six reporters on it. Wright said, 'What's the difference? Nobody who's watching knows who's first.' And from a certain point of view he was right. But once you've said that, there goes the news business."[33] GE's strategy was to cut news costs, which led it to attempt mergers with both CNN and Time Inc. in 1987. When Ted Turner desperately needed cash after his acquisition of MGM/UA, Wright pursued an "alliance" with Turner, which would have meant joint ownership of the network along with Time and Telecommunications Inc. (TCI), the cable giant that had a heavy minority stake in TBS. Turner found the money elsewhere, and the alliance never came to pass.[34] Shortly afterward, NBC established the Consumer News and Business Channel (CNBC) as an entry point into the cable news business. Since then it has set up the NBC News Channel in Charlotte, North Carolina, a right-to-work state, an indication of its desire to imitate CNN's nonunion economics. Till now the news channel has served to supply NBC affiliates, but it is positioned to become the core production center for a twenty-four-hour news network. NBC's involvement in Visnews is less clear since Reuters took full control, but this may yet be an avenue for international expansion.

Cap Cities/ABC has clear ambitions to become a major global media company. In 1987, ABC sold $75 million of news and entertainment product overseas. Cap Cities/ABC already has the base in U.S. cable that GE/NBC has been actively seeking, holding a majority of the sports channel ESPN, and substantial stakes in the Arts & Entertainment (A&E) and Lifetime cable networks. ABC sees itself as a global *media* corporation more than its rivals. Its 80 percent ownership of WTN and a major exchange agreement with Japan's NHK TV position it as the

Big Three player most likely to pursue a global news audience. During the network cutbacks from 1985 onward, Cap Cities/ABC cut 300 people from its news staff of 1,450.[35] But more than its network counterparts, Cap Cities was committed to having a viable international news-gathering organization when the cutting was done.

Despite the international ambitions of GE and Cap Cities, both networks still make the lion's share of their profits in the United States. News and bureau-sharing agreements with overseas agencies lower the fixed costs of maintaining a news service that offers worldwide coverage to an American market, although these relationships are still very fluid. It seems probable that Cap Cities and GE will turn their sights to the world news market. But for now, the only U.S. company that is aggressively pursuing an international *news* strategy is CNN.

CNN International

The development of CNN in 1980 began the transformation of the international television news market into a (potential) international audience. Almost from its inception, CNN founder Ted Turner has had an international vision for his network that reflects his personal ambition as well as his growing interest in world ecology and nuclear disarmament. In a 1983 address to the National Academy of Television Arts and Sciences, Turner said he was more concerned with contributing to "the salvation of life on earth" than making money on CNN's international ventures.[36] And in 1982 he told *Time*: "I want to start dealing with issues like disarmament, pollution, soil erosion, population control, alternative energy sources."[37] Turner's interest in global ecology and disarmament drove CNN toward Moscow and Beijing. At first glance, the Soviet Union and China did not offer the greatest commercial opportunities for a U.S. television network. But Turner's internationalism was coupled with a shrewd understanding of a changing international news market, well before any of his competitors. He understood that the international news market would be limited to several major organizations, that the horizon for becoming a "player" was short, and that penetration of all world markets was a prerequisite for success.

In 1980, CNN began transmission via satellite to Japan at the request of TV Asahi, which soon became a CNN affiliate. Bureaus were quickly established in Rome, London, Tel Aviv, Cairo, and Tokyo. CNN Europe began overseas service in 1985, and was renamed CNN International. In 1987, CNNI began transmitting to eighty thousand British cable households via eight cable systems. By 1988, a Latin-American feed was added. That same year, CNN signed an agreement with the Soviet Union, allowing it to transmit on the Soviet satellite Statsionar 12, which extended its scope to the Soviet Union, the Middle East, and Africa.

In 1987, CNN extended its international commitment with the launch of "World Report," a separate division within CNN that collects broadcasts from 170 international broadcasters and packages them for daily rebroadcast on both CNN and CNNI. "World Report" plays a dual function within the CNN organization. It is both a program and international affiliate relations bureau. CNN vice president Stuart Loory was chosen by Ted Turner to start up "World Report." "In the mid-1980s Ted did some traveling in the developing countries and wherever he went he heard what at that time was the traditional UNESCO argument, that all of the news flowed from rich to poor, industrial to developing, north to south," Loory recalls. "He convinced himself that what he was hearing was correct and he came back and said we've got to do something about it. And he developed the idea, a program in which everybody got a chance."[38]

Loory says that Turner was heavily influenced by the debate over the New World Information and Communication Order, but the difficulty was in defining the ground rules: "We had a discussion in the beginning over how much time to give broadcasters from various countries. And for a while there was a concept that you gave the bigger countries more time than the smaller countries. So we played around with various formulas, and finally I said to Ted, 'How do we define bigness?'" Loory had his staff draw up a list of the top ten nations in the world in a range of categories: population, land mass, gross national product, GNP per capita, military expenditures. The only two nations that consistently ranked in the top ten were the United States and the Soviet Union. The "World Report" staff decided to compromise: All reports would be limited to three minutes, and the large nations would be limited in their monthly contributions. Loory says Turner was, in Turner's words, very concerned "to differentiate the big countries from the islands" and create equality of access.

According to current executive producer Donna Mastrangelo, the only editing of "World Report" is for obvious problems with production values—bad edits, tape, audio—or when a report's English is not understandable. "I don't want to Americanize the reports; that's the whole philosophy of this program. It's the news from the perspective of these broadcasters." She says of Turner's decision to launch the program, "He wanted something on CNN that would not be the Western media. Why should we be the ones deciding what is on the air, especially if we are going to be a global network?"[39]

Although there is no formal censorship of content, "World Report" contributors want their pieces to be "like CNN." This is the only international rebroadcast of material for most "World Report" affiliates, and they want to put on their best face. Some critics have charged that since many "World Report" contributors are government owned or controlled, that the program operates under a form of virtual censorship. Christine Ockrent, a senior correspondent for Radio Television France (RTF), says CNN is "a U.S. channel with a global vocation, but which sees the world through an American prism. . . . When CNN's footage is not homemade in the U.S., it is homemade in some other country. That's not being international."[40]

When a controlled national broadcast network contributes to "World Report," it does reflect the point of view of its government. Ockrent's criticism, however, like similar charges from the BBC, presumes that Western news-gathering organizations represent a neutral point of view, a presumption disputed by scholars, journalists, and governments throughout the Third World. This fundamental difference of viewpoint was the impetus for the movement of the so-called less developed countries (LDCs) for a New World Information and Communication Order during the 1970s and 1980s. The LDCs criticized what they saw as the one-way flow of information from the West to the Third World. Western governments, in turn, reacted to what they perceived as threats to the free flow of information. This debate has been eclipsed, if not suspended, in recent years, because of a strong Western counterattack in the United Nations.[41] Whatever the outcome of the debate, reporting about the LDCs is now anchored in the emerging world news system. The news agencies, CNN, and BBC WSTV are the television arenas in which the Third World will be represented, to itself and to the rest of the world. If CNN's dependence on its affiliates creates a refracted prism of national viewpoints, it has also created a unique international forum of public opinion that offers more equal access to nations outside the Western media orbit.

By 1989, CNN was the only one of the four major U.S. television organizations to regularly distribute outside of the nation's borders. CNN was available in nearly 120 nations, including all of Europe and Japan, and much of China, the Soviet Union, the Middle East, Africa, and Latin America. While the networks were pulling back from the world (while trying to appear as if they weren't), CNN was expanding as rapidly as it could.

◆3◆
Global News in a Global Economy

I n 1987, while attending a Venice summit of the seven world economic powers, President Ronald Reagan was asked by a group of reporters whether the value of the dollar had reached its lowest point. Reagan answered, "Frankly, most of us believe that the dollar should remain stable," but he added as an aside that he felt it could go "a bit lower." After making his comments, the president went to his hotel room and turned on the television to CNN. The dollar, he learned, had plummeted immediately after his remarks had been transmitted live via satellite and aired. Fifteen minutes later, presidential spokesman Marlin Fitzwater appeared in the hotel lobby and told the CNN crew that what the president "had meant to say was that he wanted stability for the dollar." The revised version was broadcast around the world, and as quickly as the run on the dollar began, it ended.[42]

The incident in Venice exemplifies the convergence of global economics and politics in the emerging world television system. CNN's growing international influence has followed the pathways of economic globalization. Transnational investment by the United States, Europe, and Japan accelerated rapidly in the decades after World War II. By the end of the 1980s, this process had reached a critical mass. It was not just that governments, corporations, and the public had been drawn into this global web. All were more *aware* of their greater interconnection. This growing recognition of the global ties among national economies, governments, and cultures increased the demand for a world television system that would represent and interpret this interconnection.

Growing economic complexity has also created a greater need for information. Global corporations have manufacturing facilities around the world, creating links between world currency and stock markets.

Governments, central banks, and financial institutions, as well as manufacturing and trading corporations, need immediate news of world events to predict and control their international financial environment.

Such an economic need for information, of course, was not new. As early as the eighteenth century, mercantile traders relied on financial broadsheets for timely information just as nineteenth-century clients of Reuters and Havas depended on the telegraph. What has changed is the international economic environment. The primary unit of production and exchange is the transnational corporation operating in a global economy. The global economy makes the world television system possible, by giving direct economic value to a twenty-four-hour information source.

Today, the political lives of nation states are more directly and visibly intertwined with the world economy. Global currency movements, formerly reported primarily in the financial pages of the *Wall Street Journal* and the *New York Times*, now end up in world television headlines. The world news system creates a new awareness of economic interdependency among citizens, and in so doing politicizes the world economy.

Although world television is still undergoing radical change, its outlines are beginning to emerge. It is a mix of private corporations and national broadcasting systems; it combines English language networks that cross the globe and regional satellite broadcasters that reach out to specific language communities. It is a patchwork of corporate and political alliances. In the future, there will likely be two, possibly three, networks reaching every continent. CNN is one; the BBC's World Service Television is the only other organization that is actively building an international television network. Both of these fully global networks transmit in English, with additional channels dubbed into vernacular languages. Because English is established as the international language of business and diplomacy, it is easy to overlook the implications of the de facto establishment of English as the language of an emerging world forum of information and public opinion.

Outside of the English-speaking world, and some of Western Europe and Japan, English remains a language of elites. To the extent that an English language world television system becomes the medium for global opinion, it excludes the participation of the greater part of the world's population, including the world's middle classes. Many educated people—Russians, Chinese, Germans, Africans, Latin Americans, and others—do not use English at all, or not well enough to regularly monitor English-language television.

The de facto choice of English restricts the market for global television to the world's upper and upper-middle classes, and, of course, those whose native tongue is English. But even if international net-works can be profitable when restricted to English speakers, economies of scale are greatest when news is sold across markets. Television news-film speaks all languages. A tape of a plane crash in Thailand can be used anywhere in the world. If that tape is shown in many markets, its unit cost decreases accordingly. Today, most of the news pictures for world television still come from two London-based international television agencies, Visnews and WTN. The three major U.S. networks, as well as CNN, BBC, and ITN in Great Britain and the European national broad-casters, depend on the agencies for much of their news video. Each world news organization is fighting for access to these news agencies through special agreements or joint ventures. Because special access to the agencies allows networks to cut back independent international news gathering, the outcome of this competition will influence the cost, scope, and quality of international news coverage well into the next century.[43]

At the same time, English-language global networks are pushing out-ward, toward new markets in the world's major vernacular-language groups. The global networks could enter these markets by themselves, but this is prohibitively inefficient. They will have to find partners among the major regional, vernacular-language broadcasters. Or they will have to establish new partnerships with news-gathering organizations, in which the "local" partner exchanges its knowledge of the language, culture, market, and existing news-gathering resources for the global partner's twenty-four-hour news production skill.

Between the international networks and their local partners, a series of regionally owned and operated networks is emerging. Whether these regional networks will remain independent, or become absorbed into a broader system of rival networks, is difficult to predict. Much depends on the strength of their capital bases, the spread of new technologies, and the development of global and regional advertising markets.

The prospect of cheaper direct broadcast satellite (DBS) tech-nologies could open up large portions of the vernacular-language, middle-class markets quickly. Such technologies are being tested now. Some nations have chosen to restrict the growth of direct broadcast satel-lites in the interest of national development and sovereignty, prefer-ring to rely on cable or fiber optics. But the emergence of small, cheap DBS technology could rapidly undermine these strategies of national and cultural protection that have already been eroded by the current generation of satellite dishes.

In light of these developments, it is not surprising that global adver-tising markets are growing rapidly. Advertising already supplies half of

CNN's European revenues, $25 million in 1992. That compares to total European satellite advertising revenue of $150 million. Still, the amount of satellite advertising pales compared to estimated European television advertising revenue of $30 billion. The satellite share of total world advertising revenue is rising quickly, and that is the real economic prize for global television networks and their allies. Following is a look at just who the competitors are.

BBC World Service Television: The Empire Strikes Back

There are few national television networks less identified with advertising than the BBC. Established in 1922 as the licensed commercial monopoly of six British radio corporations, the BBC has remained perched between government control over its funding and independence ever since. Lord John Reith, BBC's first managing director, set programming standards that fit the British establishment's view of high culture as a means to improve the taste of the British middle and lower classes.[44] World Service Television inherits this tradition, but with one important difference: WSTV is funded by advertising, a first in BBC history.

World Service Television began broadcasting to Europe in April of 1991. John Tusa, managing director of BBC World Service, acknowledged at launch that the BBC is behind in the international television race that, in its own estimation, it should have led. "It is now recognized that for Britain not to have been in the international TV news business during the Gulf crisis was a major strategic error," he said.[45] The BBC also acknowledged that CNN set standards for world television during the Gulf War, standards that the BBC claims were not to its liking.

WSTV chief executive Christopher Irwin fired the opening shot across CNN's bow: "CNN is brilliant reportage, I'm more dubious about its journalism." Irwin told the *New York Times*, "One danger is if you go to a press conference and turn on a camera and think that's journalism. It's not." BBC executives claim they will take a more international approach than CNN does. BBC director Michael Checkland expanded on this: "CNN's strength is the strength of America. It's a window for the world on the most powerful and influential country on the planet, as well as a look at the rest of the world through that country's window. The BBC's strength is the range and depth of its coverage and its international tradition."[46]

WSTV's European channel has carried a mixture of entertainment and news from BBC's 1 and 2 channels in Great Britain. In June 1992, WSTV announced it would split its channel into two, one carrying entertainment and the other news. The European channel is broadcast in English to some

1.25 million subscribers, but it has a much greater reach. Some national broadcasters, including several in Eastern Europe, are carrying WSTV, with an approximate viewership of twenty-six million.

In October 1991, WSTV started broadcasting its Asian edition in a joint venture with HutchVision, a Hong Kong-based multichannel direct satellite broadcast network that operates a package of advertising-supported entertainment channels under the banner of Star TV. The WSTV Asian service is broadcast in English, with Cantonese and Mandarin Chinese available on separate language tracks. The Star package, which includes BBC, a sports channel, and Music Television (MTV), is carried on AsiaSat, which reaches thirty-eight countries with a total population of 2.7 billion (the actual number of viewers is probably much smaller—in the tens of millions—restricted to those with access to cable or DBS.). WSTV transmits a five-minute insert into its Asia feed at the end of each news hour. According to Irwin: "We've had a good response to our Asian bulletins. We are beefing them up, to concentrate and focus on the subregions."[47] WSTV's Asian coverage via Star extends east to west from Israel to Taiwan and north to south from Mongolia to the Philippines. WSTV is beginning World Service Japan, a joint venture with Nissho Iwai, Japan's seventh-largest trading company. The operation is 80 percent Japanese owned.

In 1992, WSTV began telecasting on the South African M-Net satellite, which covers all of Africa. The joint venture is now selling decoders throughout Africa and will also be rebroadcast on several African national television services. Irwin says he intends to be in every continent by the end of 1993, by which time he also expects to be telecasting in the United States. In October 1992, WSTV entered into a joint operating agreement with the Canadian Broadcasting Corporation (CBC). The CBC will carry a nightly half-hour WSTV newscast, as well as fifteen-minute updates in the late evening.[48]

Joint ventures are the core of WSTV's strategy for international expansion. "We believe in joint ventures. It allows us to tailor the service according to our partner's schedules," says Irwin. "The essential difference between us and CNN is that we rely very much on our regional partners for news. We franchise great chunks, which allows us to vary our service both in funding and content."

Irwin says the second great difference between WSTV and CNN is the BBC heritage. "CNN has a fine record. Our strength is in the joint resources of the BBC. We have some 260 correspondents and bureaus. Our depth of access is greater. The amount of material built specifically for us is greater. We generally have more product designed for an international market. CNN's output is small compared to ours for an overseas audience." Irwin claims that 75 percent of WSTV material is produced exclusively for international distribution; only 25 percent has already been shown on BBC's domestic services.[49]

WSTV's British imperial legacy gives it a cultural leg up on CNN in some markets. Director Checkland says that 80 percent of viewers in India with access to international channels watch WSTV, seven times the number for CNN.[50] WSTV has been picked up for twenty-four-hour rebroadcast to the Gulf region by the national television service of Bahrain, a former British protectorate, and is popular in areas of current or former British influence, including Hong Kong. Irwin claims that WSTV will have a long-term advantage over CNN because it is more cosmopolitan: "Historically, the Atlanta world view is narrower than the BBC world view," he said, adding, "BBC World Service Radio has attempted to build up a genuinely world perspective. It's only incidental that it is headquartered in London."

World view aside, WSTV expansion is constrained by two important elements: finance and political control. Unlike the parent BBC, WSTV is not directly supported by the national license fee, a tax on each television sold. It must pay its own way through joint ventures, subscription fees, and advertising. In 1991-92, WSTV returned a reported operating loss of £3.8 million, almost $7 million, which was charged against the BBC Home Services Group. BBC claims the losses were due to exceptional startup costs. It remains unclear precisely where this deficit financing comes from, if not the British government.

The BBC's overall expansion plans are formally limited by the need to obtain joint-venture partners to cover the full cost of expansion in each new market before it can begin broadcasting, a significant contrast to CNN's historical policy: Expand first, and find the money later. Irwin claims this is an advantage: "Ted [Turner] rather likes to take risks on the market responding. Our joint ventures are a valuable thing." Both Irwin and Checkland emphasize that speed is of the essence for WSTV, yet the project can only move as quickly as prior financing allows. Critics within and outside the BBC are worried that WSTV will become a vehicle for the broader commercialization of the BBC at home, a fear reinforced by Conservative party advocates of limited privatization.

Other political problems are more subtle. Checkland is selling WSTV to the British government as a way to extend British cultural influence: "It is very important to spread our traditions around the world." But in the countries that WSTV hopes to enter, it must stress its impartiality and cultural neutrality. In Irwin's words, Bush House, World Service's home, is "like a cosmopolitan temple of truth. It is built on a diversity of cultures, a multiplicity of nations, a kaleidoscope of beliefs."[51]

Historically, the BBC has maintained an air of high culture, and high-mindedness. But it has also been a force for the extension of British cultural and political influence throughout the world. BBC World Service Radio bound the commonwealth together culturally. As the torch in international news passes from radio to television, BBC WSTV will attempt to carry on that global mission.

CNN's Robert Ross responds bluntly to the BBC's cultural claims: "BBC likes to say that their network is strong on analysis, and they'll spend ten minutes explaining to people the background, the implications, and the history. We don't do that. We give them three minutes of 'here's what's happened.' They criticize us for what we do, and we find their style quite condescending and supercilious."[52]

As part of the BBC, WSTV comes under political scrutiny. The WSTV experiments with advertising will inevitably be drawn into the parliamentary debate over the extension of the BBC's charter, when it comes up for renewal in 1996. Despite the World Service's reputation for fairness and balance, it remains an arm of the British government. BBC supporters point to its performance during the Suez crisis of 1956 as the high point of editorial independence, when the BBC allowed the Labour opposition access to the airwaves over the objections of the Conservative government. But critics point to its ambiguous coverage of other news under government pressure, including Northern Ireland and the Falklands-Malvinas War. And during the Gulf War the BBC, like its U.S. counterparts, sanitized video from Iraq. BBC Radio went even further, banning sixty-seven songs, including "Give Peace a Chance."[53]

WSTV will certainly be one of the dominant English language world news networks. Despite the sniping, this seems fine with both CNN and WSTV executives. According to Checkland, "There's room for both CNN and the BBC WSTV in a market that's just beginning to open up. Of course, we'll be in competition, but we're not offering the same product." Replies CNNI's vice president Peter Vesey: "Our feeling is that the competition is good for us and good for the BBC."

Regional News

While CNN and WSTV compete directly on the global stage, regional news organizations are jockeying for position in Europe, Latin America, Asia, and the Middle East. Some of the regionals are potential international competitors; others are restricted to a single continent or language group. Some are public service broadcasters with a political or cultural mission, others commercial enterprises. The world news system will eventually consist of a series of alliances and joint ventures between the international networks and regionals, and perhaps a series of consortia among the regionals themselves.

The rise, fall, and rise of NHK. The largest, and potentially most significant organization on the border of the world news system is Nippon Hoso Kyokai, Japan's national public service broadcaster. In December 1991, NHK publicly abandoned plans for its own worldwide twenty-four-hour news service that was to compete with CNN and BBC. The planned Global News Network (GNN) would have given Japan an international voice equal to its world economic position. Former NHK head Keiji Shima, a strong advocate of the "internationalization" of Japanese broadcasting, proposed the service in 1990, and it was propelled forward in 1991 during the Gulf War. After NHK relied on CNN, which it rebroadcasts on one of its channels, for the bulk of its Gulf War coverage, Shima, a former newsman, publicly complained that CNN was "trying to force U.S. news on the rest of the world." GNN was abandoned when Shima was forced out of office after charges that he lied to the Japanese Diet about his whereabouts during the failed launching of an NHK satellite. His successor, NHK chairman Mikio Kawaguchi, announced that "setting up GNN is out of the question." Kawaguchi said NHK could not afford to spend $800 million a year on GNN.

GNN would have provided eight hours of daily programming specializing in coverage of Asia. Eight additional hours would have been provided by a European partner, and another eight hours from the United States. Great Britain's BBC and ITN, France's TF-1, and ABC held discussions with NHK, but no final agreement was ever reached (although ABC did reach a separate agreement with NHK for a broad exchange of programming). All broadcasts would have been in English, and GNN headquarters would have been in New York to distinguish GNN from NHK's Japanese news-gathering operations. CNN's Ed Turner maintains that NHK's close relationship with Japan's ruling Liberal Democratic party made it difficult to find partners: "NHK fell on its face because it was attempting to sell ABC a chamber of commerce news service."[54] There was also reported resistance from Asian nations that suffered under Japanese colonial rule during World War II, several of which restrict Japanese satellite broadcasting because of fear of cultural domination.

The GNN plan would have built on existing NHK programming. NHK airs eight hours a day of English-language programming in Japan, and has begun offering Japanese news to the United States, primarily through "Today's Japan," a daily program aired on PBS affiliates. NHK is also broadcasting eight hours a day of programming to Europe on the Astra satellite. Robert Ross, who is in charge of international operations for Turner Broadcasting System, claims that the GNN plan was only one part of a comprehensive Japanese broadcasting strategy: first, to communicate to Japanese businessmen throughout the world; second, to present the official Japanese point of view through an English-language service; third, and perhaps least important for the present, to have a presence in the emerging world news system. The original GNN plan built on the first two legs, which already exist; only the third has been abandoned for the time being.

NHK's managing director for the United States, Kunio Irisawa, who was a part of the GNN planning group, says the plan was postponed for a lack of partners. He explains that as a public broadcaster, NHK could not afford to bear the load itself. Irisawa says that only the European Broadcasting Union (EBU), the European Community (EC) regional consortium, responded positively. But he says that NHK has decided to strengthen its Asian network rather than abandon GNN completely. A new Asian Center has been set up in Japan, staffed primarily with Japanese personnel, with bureaus in Singapore, Bangkok, Jakarta, Manila, Sydney, New Delhi, Hanoi, Phnom Penh, and Vladivostok. "The first step of the new Global News Network is to strengthen our own network in Asia. The second step is to send materials to the world. We are studying how to do that," Irisawa explained. News will be packaged at the Asian Center and put up on satellite for anyone to use. Because of its comprehensive presence in Asia, Irasawa believes NHK can supply news of Asia to the rest of the world: "We understand Asian broadcasters, and they need an Asian service." [55]

Europe. There are two satellite news efforts in Europe today, one wholly public, the other entirely commercial: Euronews, a project of the EC, and Sky News, owned by Rupert Murdoch's News Corporation. Euronews is a consortium of twelve EC state-owned broadcasters, plus the authorities of Egypt, Finland, Greece, and Monaco. The network will undoubtedly be joined by members of the former East bloc. Euronews expects to begin satellite broadcasting in five languages in 1993—English, French, German, Italian, and Spanish—to about twenty-three million homes in Europe, with spillover to the Middle East and North Africa. In July 1992, the EC agreed to provide funds to start up a sixth, Arabic-language channel at the same time. Each channel will have common pictures, with a separate language voice track.

Discussion of a European alternative to CNN began in 1988. As with WSTV and GNN, Euronews was given its impetus by CNN's coverage of the Gulf War. "CNN showed Europeans how powerful a satellite news network can be," says Patrick Olivier, director of Audiovisual

Eureka, an EC intergovernmental broadcast agency. The major participating organizations—Antenne 2 and FR 3 of France, RAI of Italy, ARD and ZDF of Germany, and RTVE of Spain—were somewhat embarrassed at their dependence on CNN during the war. The EC has agreed to fund one quarter of the projected $50 million budget for five years, through the European Broadcasting Union. The rest will come from advertising and sponsorships. Euronews will piggyback its operations on the EBU, which operates a European news clearinghouse.[56]

Euronews is building on the CNN model. It will operate as a wire service, with a stripped down staff of two hundred, building on existing EBU resources. It is not seriously expected to challenge CNN or WSTV in the world news market, or even, during major events, in Europe. Euronews is significant as a cultural and political enterprise. It was born from the recognition that a world trading bloc, the EC, cannot function when it is dependent on others for news and information. Euronews may end up competing with at least some of its members' national services, as they enter into partnerships with other world television networks.

At the other end of the European spectrum is Rupert Murdoch's Sky News, the news service of his Sky channel, which began broadcasting in 1984. Sky News is a purely commercial enterprise launched in 1991 (Sky merged with British Satellite Broadcasting later that year to become British Sky Broadcasting, BSB.) Its apparent political goal, if any, is to expand Murdoch's base as an international press lord, and its style is much closer to the Fleet Street tabloids, than the *London Times*. Sky News quickly became popular with politicians and journalists and provided a popular alternative to the state-owned agencies. Sky was licensed in Luxembourg, and launched on the popular Astra satellite. Despite losing money, the merged BSB has approximately 2.35 million subscribers and continues to grow in Europe, where it is received via direct satellite and on cable. Murdoch's Fox Network in the United States is expanding its news operations, which will give Sky News another major outlet.[57]

Vernacular broadcasting. As Euronews begins broadcasting in 1993, it will join several regional satellite broadcasters that are aiming at specific language communities. The most significant is the Middle East Broadcasting Center (MBC), headquartered in London, which has targeted some 300 million Arabic-speaking viewers in the Gulf region, the Indian subcontinent, and Africa. MBC was started by Walid al-Ibrahim, the brother-in-law of King Fahd of Saudi Arabia, as a Western-style direct broadcast satellite network to the Arab world. There is no doubt about MBC's model. According to Stephen Marney, MBC's head of news:

"When they hired me, they said 'Steve, we want CNN in Arabic.'"[58] MBC employs about two hundred people; the news is written by English-speaking journalists whose scripts are translated into Arabic.

MBC is carried on the national broadcasting networks of Bahrain, Kuwait, and Morocco, where it competes directly with Egypt's satellite channel, the current leader in the Arab world, and the nightly newscasts of national broadcast authorities. One 1992 survey in Kuwait showed 77 percent of the Kuwaiti audience watching MBC, 12 percent the Egyptian news, and 7 percent the Kuwaiti government channel. Another measure of MBC's success as an alternative source of information in the Arab world is Saudi Arabia itself. MBC's privilege to broadcast on a government channel was withdrawn in February 1992 after religious and political conservatives objected to its unveiled anchorwomen and uncensored news reports. MBC was the first Arab-language network to open a Jerusalem bureau. Its mission is to spread pro-Western Arab political views throughout the Mideast. Executive director Abdullah Masry, Saudi Arabia's chief archaeologist, says, "Slowly, we hope through MBC to prepare the air for reconciliation, to be a bridge of understanding."[59]

MBC has other aims as well. It recently acquired bankrupt United Press International for nearly $4 million, with the aim of broadening its worldwide news-gathering capacity. It provides a successful model for vernacular broadcasting, which has more than one aim. MBC is clearly a commercial venture. Its Saudi investors stand to profit handsomely over time, as MBC provides the only alternative to religious and state-controlled broadcasting in the Arab world. But MBC is also a political instrument for extending Saudi influence in particular, and pro-Western views more generally, throughout the Arab world. It will be a force for political and cultural liberalization as its influence spreads. MBC is negotiating to expand into the United States, with the East Coast, Chicago, and Detroit its primary targets. According to Nicholas Hart, head of public relations for the center, there are approximately 2.5 million Arabic speakers in the United States.[60]

The Jordanian National Broadcast Authority hopes to compete with MBC starting in 1993. The government-owned broadcaster is currently looking for space on a satellite transponder that would allow it to begin a pan-Arabic twenty-four-hour news channel.[61]

Other national and commercial broadcasters have either begun regional satellite broadcasting or are actively exploring vernacular networks. Televisa of Mexico offers satellite service to much of Spanish-speaking Latin America, as well as Europe. France's largest broadcaster, TF-1, is actively considering a French-language channel to be launched throughout Europe, the Middle East, and Africa. And there are at least three separate efforts under way to develop a German-language channel for central Europe. Many of these channels will either adopt the CNN model or actively ally themselves with CNN. As the regional vernacular broadcasters fill out the gaps in the world news system, some system of multiple alliances is almost inevitable. Exactly what those relationships will look like is almost impossible to predict. It does seem clear, however, that CNN will play a major role in building the regional networks.

CNN International and the Future of World Television

As world news competition intensifies, CNN is being pushed to concentrate on its international interests. CNN president Tom Johnson says, "Our vision is global. During the next five years, our highest priority will be given to the expansion of the CNN International network itself. Beyond that, we look to establish some new strategic alliances which may enable us to serve in the language of the regions such as Germany, Japan, and Russia. Our aspiration is to be able to report from virtually any point on the globe, to every point on the globe."[62] Although CNN is telecasting in English, both Johnson and Ted Turner have set expansion into vernacular networks as a high priority.

As head of TBS International, Robert Ross is responsible for making the business of CNNI and its vernacular affiliates work. As he explains, "There may be room for one or two, even three, global English-language networks. But clearly there's room for some regional ones. There's going to be a Spanish-language network in South America, there's going to be a news network in Japan in Japanese, there's probably going to be a French one which will go into French West Africa, and there will probably be an Arabic one. And our long-term thinking is to try to take a 30 to 40 percent interest in each of these, help them set it up and operate it, and at the same time to make each one a news supplier to the others, thus lowering news-gathering costs."[63]

The plan may be ahead of schedule. In July 1992, TBS changed its experimental Moscow channel into a permanent presence in a joint venture with the Moscow Independent Broadcasting Company (MIBC), the first independent station in Moscow supported by advertising. MIBC director Eduard Sagalaev was the director general of former, state-owned Ostankino TV. MIBC has been broadcasting CNNI for two hours a day since May 1992. The new channel will carry CNN and will also feature other Turner entertainment channels. CNN's role in Russia goes back to Turner's courting of the Soviets in the early 1980s, and to CNN's role during the coup attempt, which further enhanced its credibility with Russian journalists. CNNI vice president Peter Vesey says, "A lot of Soviet officials have come to this country to try to figure out how we do this sort of thing because they'd like to start doing it themselves as they look toward a free and independent news business."[64]

CNN has been sending a Spanish-language feed, Noticiero Telemundo, to Latin America since 1988. But its most important targets for vernacular networks are Germany and Japan. Johnson talks of a "strategic alliance" with TV Asahi in Japan, citing a shared bureau in Bangkok and Asahi's substantial payments to air CNN "World Report" in Japan. Johnson says CNN is discussing a direct broadcast satellite venture in Japan and he refers to "active exploration of a German channel." Ross explains that ventures for something like a "Deutschland News Network-DNN" are already under active consideration. This, he says, would be a "hybrid network. Instead of appealing to 3 percent of the German audience, it might appeal to 25 percent." CNN has submitted an application for a German-language cable news channel, CNN-Deutschland, in the southwestern state of Baden-Wurttemberg with German public service broadcaster ZDF. One barrier may be the German State Broadcasting Treaty, which forbids public service broadcasters to get involved in private advertising-supported ventures aimed at a German audience. Regardless of the outcome of the CNN-ZDF application, it seems probable that it will trigger a German debate over public service broadcaster participation in vernacular satellite ventures.[65]

CNNI is actively expanding its international news content. Johnson says that while CNN in the United States will contain 60 to 70 percent domestic news and 30 to 40 percent international, the ratio on CNNI will be reversed. When asked whether an international channel with such a high U.S. content will be of interest, he responds, "We cannot ignore the fact that there is still a tremendous demand among those who view us for United States news. Not only from U.S. citizens, but from people around the world." Johnson says the best of CNNI will be carried on CNN's U.S. broadcasts, but whether CNNI in its entirety will be available is uncertain: "There may be a market for CNNI on a limited basis in the United States, particularly for all those who have great international news interests. But I don't yet know how large that market will be and whether there will be sufficient advertisers for it. Ted [Turner] generally likes that idea." For now, CNNI will continue to appeal to a relatively elite world audience. "CNNI in English is going to appeal to 2, 3, 4 percent of the market," says Ross. "Maybe 10 percent in some places like Amsterdam, which has an English fluent upscale segment of the population."

In 1992, CNNI finished an ambitious upgrading of its worldwide satellite system and is now on the major satellites in every region of the world:

Astra in Europe; Arabsat for the Middle East, Africa, and the Indian sub-continent; Superbird in Japan and East Asia; and Indonesia's Palapa for Southeast Asia and the Pacific. WSTV has just moved into Japan and Africa and is still discussing plans for North and South America. NHK is only beginning to build a world satellite network.

At a time when the U.S. networks are cutting back their worldwide news-gathering efforts, CNN is expanding rapidly. In 1992, it opened new bureaus in Rio, Amman, Bangkok, and New Delhi. Peter Vesey says that regional production centers are being planned for Tokyo and Mexico City and will be integrated into CNNI international coverage now anchored in London. An African center in Johannesburg is also under consideration.

CNN's head start will give it an enormous financial advantage in the two critical areas of revenue and cost. First, it is relying on the same "dual revenue stream"—revenues from both subscription fees and advertising—that made CNN successful in the United States. Cable television is growing throughout the world, and DBS dishes are becoming smaller and cheaper. CNN's satellite network means that it can readily exploit opportunities in both areas as subscription possibilities multiply. And while the international advertising market is still relatively small, it is expanding at an enormous rate. In 1987, CNNI received only $40 thousand in European ad revenue; by 1992 this had grown to $25 million, and Ross says this is still a tiny piece of a potential $3.4 billion market in Europe alone.

Unlike the domestic dual-income stream, international revenues come from five sources. In addition to advertising and subscription fees, CNNI receives revenue from hotels (more than thirteen hundred in Europe alone), from broadcasters who pay for it as a news service, and from institutions that subscribe to it as a wire service, including newspapers, governments, banks, and multinational corporations. No single source would be able to support an international service, but all five made growth possible during the early years. Ross says advertising alone will pay for CNNI's European operation within two years.

CNN's second competitive advantage is cost. Establishing an international news service entails a high fixed investment. The cost of expanding existing news organizations—CNNI, WSTV, NHK—is incremental because some of their fixed costs have already been paid by the parent organization. However, of all the international organizations, CNN has by far the largest subscriber base—sixty million households in the United States—which gives it an enormous advantage over its competitors. Rupert Murdoch's Sky News, for example, is trying to produce a similar amount of news on a less ambitious scale with a base of two million subscribers. In 1990, producing an hour of CNN cost approximately $20,000, an hour of Headline News about $4,000, and only $400 added cost for an hour of CNNI. In contrast, the base cost for an hour of BBC programming in 1990 was approximately £55,000, or $80,000, four times CNN's hourly cost, while the BBC was serving only twenty-two million households, about one-third of CNN's domestic viewer base. Although WSTV's costs per hour are much lower, resting on the existing BBC programming and news-gathering base, it may have a difficult time competing with CNN over the long run without direct subsidies from the British government.

Although CNN still operates independently, its two largest investors are the U. S. cable giant, Telecommunications Inc. (TCI), and Time-Warner, which together hold a stake of 7.5 percent. There is no evidence to date of editorial interference by either corporation. But Time-Warner is the largest single media enterprise in the world, with total sales in 1989 of $8.7 billion. From its base in the U.S. news and entertainment industries, Time-Warner plans to expand throughout the world. Ironically, in light of its stake in CNN, Time-Warner has invested in a German-language vernacular channel, N-TV, headquartered in East Berlin, along with several other joint ventures including the multinational Bertelsmann media group and a third German channel. Despite speculation that CNN would become Time-Warner's stalking horse, it appears Time-Warner is looking toward its own vernacular news channels. To further complicate matters, CNN has had its own discussions with N-TV, possibly creating a three-way alliance.[66]

Whether ABC, NBC, and CBS want to be global media organizations or will remain content to divide up two-thirds of the news market in the United States remains unclear. As stated earlier, there are a few signs that the networks—shaken by CNN—are interested in exporting their news outside the United States. (NBC has moved toward a twenty-four-hour cable news network, with its CNBC and NBC News Channel, but this seems to be primarily a hedge against domestic cable competition.) In fact, the Big Three are continuing to scale back their international coverage. Bureaus have been closed or consolidated throughout the world even while CNN expands. Joint operating agreements with foreign broadcasters are oriented more toward cutting costs than expanding coverage. Former NBC News president Reuven Frank characterized the Big Three approach to news this way: "News is a commodity; it's information retrieval. It's not a matter of better or worse; you sell it at the market price. It's like wheat."[67]

NBC has given up its part ownership of Visnews, in exchange for the right to market its own video internationally. ABC continues to hold 80 percent of WTN, although it may be forced to return some portion to ITN, the original British owner. CBS is casting about for international partners, with little apparent success to date. It is possible that the ABC-NHK alliance will strengthen, as NHK proves itself a reliable news-gathering partner in its Asia venture. But this will take at least several years, during which CNNI and WSTV will continue consolidating their world markets and entering new regional ones.

If the ownership picture is uncertain, CNN's influence is not. It has dominated both the form and content of international news, either direct-ly or by influence. Virtually all of the new regional channels have described themselves as aspiring to be "like CNN." This is more startling when we remember that most areas of the world have been dominat-ed by the public service broadcasting model, in many cases exclu-sively. The CNN model emerged from the American news tradition: the Associated Press newswire "give it to me quick and give it to me straight" school of news, combined with the live propensities of local American television. When one watches the major networks' foreign coverage, espe-cially during times of crisis, they look more like CNN, rather than the other way around. CNN has forced them to go live more often and to be more aggressive news-gathering organizations or risk embarrass-ment. And according to Eason Jordan, CNN's plans are broader yet. "Up until now, we've focused on being the best program service we can be, but Ted [Turner] is absolutely determined for CNN to be a television news agency. We'll see what happens with that. There are a lot of pri-orities right now, but that's something he very much wants to do." [68]

·4·
World News and Global Diplomacy

A s is evident from events such as the Gulf War and the Tiananmen Square Massacre, the world television system has begun to supplant traditional diplomatic activity. The use of an international news system as a medium of public diplomacy is not novel: By the end of the nineteenth century, some critics were complaining of the influence of newspapers on world diplomacy. But today's system of international relations is bound together by world television in three significant ways. By creating a new awareness of economic interdependency among citizens, as already described, world television has politicized the world economy. It is also evident, by word and deed, that CNN is monitored constantly by heads of state, foreign offices, political organizations, and nongovernmental organizations around the world. It is an immediate source of diplomatic information, which not only delivers news of events, but allows an immediate avenue for governments to respond to them, long before any formal diplomatic letter can be written, much less delivered. Essentially, it can serve as a diplomatic wire service and party line that operates in real global time. By the end of 1992, CNN was seen to be the foreign policy tool of choice. Noting that CNN seemed to be the medium through which President Bush had gotten most of his news during the Persian Gulf and Soviet coup crises, Thomas L. Friedman of the *New York Times* wrote that despite the trials of transition, President-elect Clinton's foreign policy aides, armed with a television, "agree they are ready for business on the Cartesian-like principle: 'I have CNN, therefore I exist.'" [69]

World television has also begun to solidify new forces of world public opinion. The starvation of Africa, the suppression of students in China, slaughter in Bosnia—these events can no longer be represented in purely national terms by national broadcast systems. The new access to a world television system offers a programming alternative, however imperfect, against which the claims of national broadcast systems can be measured.

Perhaps most striking of all, world televison not only reflects and shapes opinion, but can actually channel events themselves. This was particuarly evident during the 1991 Soviet coup attempt. A look at just what happened might allow us to see more precisely how world television might function during future world crises.

The Soviet Coup Attempt of 1991

China coverage focused world television's spotlight on repression within the borders of a sovereign nation and telecast those events to the rest of the world, but ultimately did not prevent that repression. The Gulf War established world television as a communication system; world leaders, diplomats, and the public used the world television stage to influence and send each other messages and propagate their points of view. The attempted Soviet coup introduced a new role for world television that combined the previous two. For the first time, an act of repression was monitored by the outside world, and the act of monitoring altered, however subtly, the course of events. Although CNN's presence in the Soviet Union was not directly responsible for changing the course of the coup, it did have a demonstrable effect on its outcome. As in China, BBC World Service Radio and the Voice of Liberty combined with CNN to provide a source of outside information; but only CNN was a witness within the Soviet Union itself, transmitting to the outside world.

The major events of the coup are now well known. Soviet hard-liners, led by a group of seven plotters, seized then-Soviet president Mikhail Gorbachev while he was on vacation at his Crimean dacha. The plotters urged Gorbachev to resign, which he refused to do. However, the coup plotters acted with remarkable clumsiness and indecision. In the past, one of the first acts would have been to seize all state radio, television, and press outlets. But by 1991 the process of perestroika had decentralized the Soviet press, creating a semiformal, independent public sphere outside of direct state control and making it difficult to seize the press. This confusion led to a relatively high level of independence from previously official state media for several days after Gorbachev's seizure, creating tremendous confusion both within the USSR and in international public opinion.

During these days of indecision, the plotters were able to establish central control of the state media. However, a small radio station set up by the Moscow City Council and the Moscow University Department of Journalism, Echoes of Moscow, broadcast troop movements and other developments throughout the coup, staying on the air by continually moving the transmitter. Because of CNN's long-term bridge building with the USSR, many Soviet government, press, academic, labor, and other quasi-official organizations, as well as hotels, had satellite dishes capable of receiving CNN. An estimated hundred thousand members of the Soviet intelligentsia, the core of the state apparatus, were capable of following the coup events live, without state censorship, on CNN. In addition, a one-hundred watt UHF transmitter had been beaming a CNN test signal to Moscow, which could be captured by many ordinary citizens.[70]

Anecdotal evidence suggests that the coup plotters understood CNN's potential effect. A swing figure, Alexander Bessmertnykh, first deputy foreign minister, met with General Colin Powell at the United Nations during Gorbachev's visit in 1988. Bessmertnykh congratulated Powell on his promotion that day to four-star general. When Powell remarked that the Soviet Embassy must be reporting very quickly, Bessmertnykh laughed and replied he had seen the news on CNN in Moscow. When Powell expressed scepticism, saying CNN had only been available temporarily in the hotels during the May summit earlier that year, Bessmertnykh reportedly replied, "No, we have it there permanently. I have it in my office and I watch it all day long."[71]

On August 19, day two, Soviet tanks moved on the headquarters of parliament and it appeared that the coup would succeed. Soon-to-be Russian president Boris Yeltsin took command of the forces inside the parliament building. By monitoring Soviet broadcasts, Yeltsin and the anticoup forces knew they were cut off from official Soviet media. With parliament surrounded, Yeltsin mounted the Soviet army tanks to address the growing crowds outside the building.

He certainly knew that his message was not going out over official Soviet channels. But he and his staff also knew that CNN was continuing its live coverage from Moscow: CNN had set up a camera across from the parliament building and was sending out accounts of events in front of the parliament building. In effect, by climbing on the tanks, Yeltsin was for the first time using world television to circumvent censorship in an internal political struggle in a single nation. He knew that CNN was broadcasting his pleas for resistance and assistance, not only to the world *outside* the Soviet Union, but through CNN's satellite channels to much of the state apparatus and intelligentsia within the USSR as well. According to CNN's Loory, "A number of people have told me that CNN played an important role in gathering people to the White House [Soviet parliament] by seeing the pictures. Many people in the intelligensia have told me over and over again. Ted [Turner] heard it in May [1992]."

Peter Vesey says CNN was an indirect source of information: "People were calling their friends in the parliament building from all over the Soviet Union to say 'I'm watching CNN. I'll tell you what's going on.'" There is also anecdotal evidence that middle-level Soviet officials went to work during the crisis to watch CNN. Vesey says that sources inside the Soviet Union have told him that the pictures of resistance outside parliament were significant, but that the press conference of the coup plotters, which both CNN and Soviet television carried live, was also decisive. "People got a look at these guys, and they were all second rank, very nervous, clearly reactionary unpopular leaders who, just by their demeanor, were very nervous about what they were doing."[72]

CNN reporter Claire Shipman had commandeered a telephone line in the parliament building and was sending reports directly to Atlanta. She spoke with Yeltsin, who knew that the reports were going to the outside world and, via CNN, back into the Soviet Union.

In the United States, President Bush watched as Yeltsin sat on the tank outside parliament. Later, a senior adviser told the *Chicago Tribune* that image had been decisive: "When the president saw that, that was the key for us." Despite Yeltsin's phone messages to Washington, it was only his "visible and verifiable" television image that convinced the president that resistance to the coup was serious.[73]

In Russia, CNN was also available outside of government offices. CNN and Gostelradio (GR), the official Soviet television agency, had been experimenting with broadcasting on a UHF frequency just before the coup. Most Soviet-made televisions cannot receive UHF, but Russians who owned sets with UHF capability could watch CNN. The government was aware that CNN was being viewed and issued orders to shut down the broadcasts. Vyacheslav Misyulin, who runs the Moscow TV tower responsible for transmitting all signals, refused to obey the orders and CNN continued to be broadcast. Misyulin had a contract with GR to distribute CNN. According to Loory, "The order came over to GR to turn off CNN from Valentin Lazutkin. It went down the chain in GR till it got to the bureacracy dealing with the TV tower. Then it went back up again to Misyulin. He said he couldn't recognize it, and then it went back down, and back up again." The GR bureaucrats and Misyulin danced a slow dance of inaction, which kept CNN on the air.

While it is difficult to know yet precisely how the CNN broadcasts of Yeltsin were received and by whom, it seems probable that the general

knowledge among the coup forces, the anticoup forces, and the unde-
cided populace at large that CNN was continuing to broadcast within
the USSR contributed to the several days of additional paralysis. This gap
proved sufficient to rally successfully the anticoup forces under Yeltsin.[74]

In September 1991, Christopher Irwin, chief executive of BBC WSTV,
criticized CNN's coverage of the coup, saying: "Journalism relies at
least as much on depth of knowledge as on actuality." Irwin contrasted
BBC World Service Radio's ability to read the warning signs of the
impending coup—solemn music, the broadcasting style of earlier years.
He said, "It was a considerable time before CNN came to grips with the
full implications of what was happening. The opening moves in the coup
were not much marked by actuality. It took depth of knowledge and
experience to make a decent assessment of what was going on."[75]

BBC told us what was going on from its own point of view; CNN showed
us what was going on, solemn music and all. Former Soviet foreign minister Eduard Shevardnadze (who is now the acting president of Georgia),
writing in *Newsweek* that same month, had a somewhat different assessment. After praising Moscow journalists who deserted the coup,
Shevardnadze wrote: "Freedom of information is an inalienable aspect
of freedom and democracy. Praised be information technology! Praised
be CNN! Anyone who owned a parabolic antenna able to receive this network's transmissions had a complete picture of what was happening."[76]

The global representation of events as they occur—in "real time"—
complicates the governing of nations. As we have seen, during the
Soviet coup attempt, coup leaders monitored their own actions on
CNN. They not only knew that the outside world was witnessing events
inside the Soviet Union, they understood that their actions were being
monitored by some of their own citizens on CNN and that, furthermore,
their citizens could *see* for themselves that the outside world was
watching as well.

This fluidity of information across borders poses difficult problems
in an era of geopolitical redefinition. The formation of national borders
has always been a haphazard affair. The shape of modern Europe owes
as much to conquest and dynastic alliances as to anything that we might
call "natural" ethnic boundaries. Today, national borders are being
redrawn again, fueled by ethnic and religious nationalism. Homogeneous
national cultures give way to cross-border flows of people, languages, and
cultures, further blurring the lines of national integration, as is most evident in the former Soviet Union and central Europe.

In this world of blurring cultural and national boundaries, the
world news system will continue to exert an influence. Throughout the
modern era, nation-states have been the central arenas for "the public

sphere," places where citizens meet to discuss their common problems on equal grounds and potentially come to an agreement. In Western democracies, the representative institutions of the public sphere have been national parliaments and the media: newspapers in the nineteenth century, radio and television in the twentieth. The idea of world public opinion was largely fictional: Exchanges between nations took place through governments without addressing a world audience. For the most part, media production and consumption remained within national boundaries. With the exception of readers of elite newspapers, the members of the public in one nation did not read the same newspapers or view the same television as those in another.

The rise of the world television system is beginning to break down the partitioning of public spheres by national boundaries. Before the 1980s, international television news organizations came together at the sites of spectacular or momentous events: coronations, the Olympics, summits.[77] But these international events were covered by national news organizations for their national audiences. With the rise of CNN and the development of international alliances among national broadcasters, world television began to constitute a common space during less exceptional moments, like the Group of Seven meeting in Venice. As we look toward the next century, we can say with certainty that world television will continue to grow in both scope and influence. The anchor networks, CNN and the BBC, will consolidate their international positions and find new vernacular partners. Twenty-four-hour news will be available in virtually every nation, and every major language group. But it is conceivable that the very growth of the world system could undermine its power as an international public sphere. In looking to the future, we might look to the recent past: Before cable rose in the 1980s to fragment the national audience, the American networks were a unifying "electronic hearth" throughout the country. So too it could be that as the new anchor networks take their place alongside CNN and the BBC and vernacular networks multiply, the global audience that is just coming into existence will fragment.

Also, although these world television organizations span the globe in their coverage and their audience, they are still compromised; that is, they are still predominantly Anglo-American. They embody the cultural frameworks and the news values of their managers and owners, even if the universalistic statements of owners and managers are taken at face value. There is ample precedent to believe that organizational self-interest will be put above a vaguely articulated global interest whenever the two come in conflict.

Despite claims of global responsibility and universal outlook, the world television networks attend to their market interests first. Ted Turner has forbidden CNN employees from using the term foreign; his earliest conceptions of CNN tied it to what economists would call "external goals": disarmament, peace, and the environment. Christopher Irwin stresses the BBC's universal outlook, suggesting that it is an international agency that happens to be headquartered in London. Nevertheless, each network navigates the shifting economies of the global news markets in which it sells its information products. Each organization is a powerful transnational entity, engaged in global economic competition. CNN must turn a profit for shareholders. Public corporations, like the BBC, are under increasing pressure to show both economic and political returns on investment. Regardless of aspirations, in the end the BBC and NHK must satisfy their governments that investment in world television brings political and cultural gains in the world market of public opinion.

World television is beginning to crystallize international public opinion through event-driven issues—a process we have seen from Tiananmen to the 1992 Earth Summit on the environment in Rio. But public opinion on specific issues differs from a public policy forum, or public sphere, in which an international *agenda* might be forged. For example, environmental issues were widely discussed on world television before the Rio summit. World television played a role in mobilizing public opinion, which forced sometimes-reluctant governments to compromise national interests and those of private corporations in order to meet the environmentally-defined global public interest.

The global public interest in the world television system is just as strong. The world television system plays a significant role in determining which economic, political, and cultural issues are shared throughout the world. The history of media regulation in the United States has shown that the film and broadcast industries have attended to their private interests first, and have addressed broader public issues only under regulatory pressure. The patchwork of public and private, national and commercial interests that make up the world television system aren't likely to reach consensus regarding a global public interest standard on their own. They are less likely to enforce such a standard.

Where might this debate take place? Since the end of the cold war, the United Nations appears to have grown in stature. In mobilizing the anti-Iraq coalition through the United Nations, the United States helped bestow new legitimacy on the world organization, even if in its own national interest. The Gulf War advanced the concept of legitimate norms of international behavior that the United States bound itself to acknowledge. The Rio summit on the environment offered a framework in which nations came together to agree in principle that private interests within their boundaries could be limited to achieve international goals. In the wake of Rio, it is possible to think that a similar debate on the international public sphere might also be possible, in which all nations would come together to work out legitimate goals for an international communication system.

Such a debate has, of course, already occurred. The New World Information and Communication Order (NWICO) debate that took place in UNESCO during the 1970s and 1980s fell apart on the twin shoals of the cold war and north-south divisions. Regardless of its merits, the NWICO was caught between American and European media interests and the Western perception that the NWICO would encourage an unholy news alliance between the socialist nations and the Third World. The United States used the NWICO debate to disengage from UNESCO and to distance itself from the United Nations. The example of Rio shows that international cooperation to regulate private activity in the global interest is possible and legitimate. It holds out hope for a similar resumption of the international discussion on the shape of world news.

Of course, the world news system will continue to evolve with or without such a dialogue. It will continue to alter world politics, shape economies, and forge world public opinion. Its centers of power will remain in the West and Japan. And the north-south issues that led to the original NWICO debate will not go away. But the world television system is still being formed. This is the time to begin the discussion of a global interest in communication, while it could still make a difference.

By most accounts, CNN is the most influential television news-gathering organization in the world. If it currently is tilted toward those world elites who speak English and have access to cable or satellites, that too is changing. The citizen of Moscow or Mexico City can now watch CNN in his or her own language; those in Tokyo, Berlin, and Paris are not far behind. CNNI programs for an international elite, while CNN at home reaches a mass audience. As CNNI expands through its vernacular channels to reach a middle-level audience worldwide, its effect on international public opinion will likely grow as well. Culture and politics are becoming intertwined as they have never been before.

For now, CNN is both a U.S. network broadcasting internationally and an international network, headquartered in the United States.

That balance will shift in the coming years. As BBC World Service Television and competing regional networks expand, CNN's freedom of movement will become constrained. NHK may yet emerge as a world television power. But the period in which broadcasting was exclusively a national affair is over. The home market in television now plays much the same global role as it has in manufacturing: It is either a territory to be invaded or a base from which to expand. And that terrain will remain contested well into the twenty-first century.[78]

Notes

1. Two other events in 1989 were significant for the advance of world news, the U.S. invasion of Panama and the fall of communism in Eastern Europe. The December invasion allowed the new techniques of live news gathering to be tried out during war. This dress rehearsal for the Gulf War was significant not only for the news organizations, but for the Pentagon as well. If the Falklands/Malvinas War and invasion of Grenada had demonstrated to the U.S. military the virtue of controlling the news, the invasion of Panama allowed a field trial of these new techniques of open censorship during a live war *in an international satellite news-gathering environment.* CNN and the Big Three had learned valuable lessons about using satellite news gathering for breaking stories during the China crisis, and now the Pentagon was forced to take those lessons into account in its public relations planning for the next war.

The other event was the demise of communism in Eastern Europe, symbolized by the fall of the Berlin Wall in December 1989. This was a "set piece." The story was there to be covered, the Big Three realized that they had to be there, and stressed the importance of the event by sending their anchors to the Wall. CNN kept up but did not shine in comparison, as it had during the China story and would during the Gulf War. When the networks and CNN went head to head on a story that was there for the picking, the Big Three would still hold their own.

2. This is a schematic account of the Chinese events of 1989. For a full account of U.S. media coverage of the Beijing Spring, see Joan Shorenstein Barone Center, "Turmoil at Tiananmen: A Study of U.S. Press Coverage of the Beijing Spring of 1989," John F. Kennedy School of Government, Harvard University, 1992, from which much of this material is drawn.

3. Ibid., pp. 50-65. NBC is not mentioned here because it was not covered in the study.

4. Ibid., pp. 134-35.

5. Ibid., pp. 171-72.

6. Mark Hopkins, "Watching China Change," *Columbia Journalism Review,* October 1989, pp. 35-40.

7. Joseph Streich, "China 1989: CNN Comes of Age," *Wrap*, January/February 1990, pp. 22-24.

8. William Henry III, "Man of the Year: History as It Happens," *Time*, January 6, 1992, p. 25.

9. "Turmoil at Tiananmen," p. 188.

10. Analysis of media coverage of the Gulf War has become something of a cottage industry. There are numerous accounts of the war itself from the popular to the academic; heroic self-revelation by journalists who covered the war; analyses of public relations, censorship, and television; and scholarly articles by the score. See Thomas B. Allen, F. Clifton Berry, and Norman Polmar, *CNN: War in the Gulf* (Atlanta: Turner Publishing, 1991); Robert Wiener *Live from Baghdad* (New York: Doubleday, 1992); John R. MacArthur, *Second Front: Censorship and Propaganda in the Gulf War* (New York: Hill and Wang, 1992); Jacqueline E. Sharkey, *Under Fire: U.S. Military Restrictions on the Media from Grenada to the Persian Gulf* (Washington, D.C.: Center for Public Integrity, 1991); Douglas Kellner, *The Persian Gulf War and Television* (Boulder, Colo.: Westview Press, 1992).

11. Edwin Diamond, "How CNN Does It: Winning the Gulf War," *New York*, February 11, 1991, pp. 31-39.

12. Henry, "Man of the Year," pp. 24–25.

13. George Bush, quoted in Henry, "Man of the Year," p. 24; Richard Cheney, quoted in "CNN Grabs Spotlight in Live TV War," *Electronic Media*, January 21, 1991, p. 1; Bob Woodward, *The Commanders* (New York: Simon and Schuster, 1991), p. 370; William Webster, quoted in Henry, "Man of the Year," p. 24.

14. Allen, Berry, and Polmar, *CNN: War in the Gulf*, pp. 94, 159.

15. Stuart H. Loory, vice president, CNN, interview with author, Atlanta, August 11, 1992.

16. Robert Furnad, executive vice president, senior executive producer, CNN, interview with author, Atlanta, August 27, 1991.

17. Donna Mastrangelo, executive producer, "World Report," interview with author, Atlanta, August 26, 1991.

18. Separate viewership numbers for the two programs are not available. In the absence of hard evidence, it is fair to assume that "World Report," placed in prominent afternoon and weekend time slots, paralleled CNN average viewership during the war, which was considerably higher than its normal ratings. "International Correspondents," in early-morning and late-night time slots undoubtedly drew a minuscule viewership. Although this restricted exposure to these points of view, in the context of the virtual *absence* of nonmainstream public opinion, the offering of any substantial alternatives is significant.

19. Michael Dugan, quoted in Henry, "Man of the Year," p. 25; Bernard Gwertzman, quoted in Thomas J. Colin, "As Television Glanced off the Story, Newspapers Surrounded It," *Washington Journalism Review*, March 1991, pp. 31-33.

20. Robert Ross, vice president for international development, Turner Broadcasting System, interview with author, Atlanta, August 11, 1992.

21. Hank Whittemore, *CNN: The Inside Story* (Boston: Little, Brown, 1990), p. 23.

22. Ibid., p. 33.

23. Ibid., p. 113.

24. Loory, interview with author, August 11, 1992.

25. Christopher Sterling, "Cable and Pay Television," in Benjamin Compaine, ed., *Who Owns the Media?* 2d ed. (White Plains, N.Y.: Knowledge Industry Publications, 1982), p. 404.

26. Tony Schwartz, "The TV News, Starring Ted Turner," *New York Times,* May 25, 1980, sec. 3., p. 1.

27. Ken Auletta, *Three Blind Mice* (New York: Random House, 1991), pp. 18, 227.

28. Bill Carter, "Networks Reduce Foreign Coverage," *New York Times,* June 10, 1992, p. B-4.

29. Technically, CBS maintains an international subsidiary, CBI, which sells its pictures overseas. CBI exports so-called reality-based programming, including "CBS Evening News," "60 Minutes," and "48 Hours" to parts of Europe and Asia, but it is not considered a competitive international news agency by most observers.

30. Quotes from Teresa L. Waite, "As Networks Stay Home, Two Agencies Roam the World," *New York Times,* March 8, 1992, sec. 4, p. 5.

31. Herbert Gans, *Deciding What's News* (New York: Harper & Row, 1979); Morton Rosenblum, *Coups and Earthquakes: Reporting the World for America* (New York: Harper & Row, 1979).

32. Jeremy Tunstall, *The Media Are American* (New York: Columbia University Press, 1977).

33. Reuven Frank, former president, NBC News, interview with author, New York City, February 6, 1992.

34. Auletta, *Three Blind Mice,* p. 401.

35. Ibid., p. 210.

36. Maurine Christopher, "Videotech Update," *Electronic Media,* July 14, 1983.

37. William Henry III, "Shaking Up the Networks," *Time,* August 9, 1982, pp. 50-57.

38. Loory, interview with author, August 11, 1992.

39. Mastrangelo, interview with author, August 26, 1991.

40. Henry, "Man of the Year," p. 27.

41. For a complete account of the NWICO debate, see George Gerbner, Hamid Mowlana, and Kaarle Nordenstreng, eds., *The Global Media Debate: Its Rise, Fall, and Renewal* (Norwood, N.J.: Ablex, 1992). See also Dennis McPhail, *Electronic Colonialism* (Los Angeles: Sage, 1987).

42. "White House Clarifies Reagan Remarks on Dollar," Reuters, June 11, 1987; Robert Ross, interview with author, August 11, 1992; Lou Dobbs, senior vice president, managing editor of business news, CNN, phone interview with author, October 2, 1992; Myron Kandell, CNN business correspondent, phone interview with author, October 2, 1992.

43. Network executives and critics alike agree that international news pictures will increasingly come from the same two or three sources and that the major networks will begin to look more alike. The major networks claim that this will not affect the quality of their product because of the experience of their anchors, producers, and writers. CNN claims to offer an unmatchable twenty-four-hour canvas that can be broadcast live from anywhere in the world. But this "depth versus breadth" debate obscures some large similarities among the

Big Three and CNN. All pursue similar international stories. More often than not, CNN is first with those stories, but once they are packaged, the results do not differ significantly. When beat reporters and in-house experts interpret world events for an American audience, they tend to do so through the filters of domestic institutions. The differences are ones of style and speed. For further discussion, see Bethami A. Dobkin, "Constructing News Narratives: ABC and CNN Cover the Gulf War," in Robert E. Denton, ed., *Media and the Gulf War* (New York: Praeger, forthcoming). Also see Timothy E. Cook, "Domesticating a Crisis: Washington Newsbeats and International Network News after the Iraqi Invasion of Kuwait," paper delivered at the International Communication Association, Miami, Florida, May 1992.

44. Philip Schlesinger, *Putting Reality Together: BBC News* (London: Routledge, 1987).

45. Steven Prokesch, "BBC's Global Challenge to CNN," *New York Times*, October 28, 1991, p. D9.

46. Jess Bravin, "BBC Expands World News Coverage," *Los Angeles Times*, April 17, 1992, p. F-7.

47. Christopher Irwin, chief executive, BBC World Service Television, phone interview with author, July 27, 1992.

48. Richard Siklos, "The BBC-CTV Deal that Wasn't to Be," *Financial Post*, October 8, 1992, p. 14.

49. Christopher Irwin, interview with author, July 27, 1992. Irwin cites the combined correspondent/bureau figure of 260. Bureaus can be defined as a single radio correspondent, or even a stringer. If we define bureaus by standard television definitions of correspondent, photographer, and sound person, the number of BBC bureaus worldwide would drop considerably.

50. Heather Hartt, "BBC Director Forecasts Global Television Village," *The Hollywood Reporter*, April 21, 1992.

51. Christopher Irwin, "Address to the Delhi Press Club," New Delhi, India, March 5, 1992.

52. Ross, interview with author, August 11, 1992.

53. For Northern Ireland, see Schlesinger, *Putting Reality Together*; for the Falklands, see Sharkey, *Under Fire*, pp. 61-66; and for the Gulf War, see Philip Taylor, "Crisis in the Gulf: TV's Key Role in Battle for Hearts and Minds," *The Independent* (London), February 19, 1991, p. 3, and "Ally Watch," *Los Angeles Times*, January 26, 1991, p. B5.

54. Ed Turner, executive vice president for news gathering, CNN, comments at "The Changing Face of News," a seminar of the International Radio and Television Society, New York, February 6, 1992; David E. Sanger, "NHK of Japan Ends Plan for Global News Service, *New York Times*, December 9, 1991, p. C8.

55. Kunio Irisawa, managing director, NHK, United States, phone interview with author, July 20, 1992.

56. Patrick Olivier, quoted in Douglas Lavin, "Europeans Put CNN on Notice: Stay Tuned for Euronews in '93," *Atlanta Constitution*, February 26, 1992, p. C8; for information on funding see Alan Riding, "European Channel Takes a Stab at CNN," *New York Times*, February 24, 1992, p. C8.

57. Euromedia Research Group, *The Media in Western Europe* (Newbury Park, Calif.: Sage, 1992), pp. 250-51.

58. Peter Waldman, "Western-Style TV Fare Is Dished Out to Arab Viewers via MBC Satellite," *Wall Street Journal*, March 5, 1992, p. A10.

59. Survey results in Youssef M. Ibrahim, "TV Is Beamed at Arabs, the Arabs Beam Back," *New York Times*, March 4, 1992, p. A4; Abdullah Masry, quoted in Waldman, "Western-Style TV Fare Is Dished Out to Arab Viewers via MBC Satellite."

60. Nicholas Hart, head of public relations, Middle East Broadcasting Center, phone interview with author, November 12, 1992.

61. "Jordan Plans Panarabic TV Channel in 1993," *Middle East Communications Magazine*, September 1992.

62. Tom Johnson, president, CNN, interview with author, Atlanta, May 27, 1992.

63. Richard Ross, interview with author, May 27, 1992.

64. Peter Vesey, vice president, CNN International, interview with author, Atlanta, May 27, 1992.

65. Wolfgang Koschnick, "CNN Teams Up with ZDF," *Cable and Satellite Express*, August 7, 1992.

66. For Time-Warner data, see Anthony Smith, *The Age of Behemoths: The Globalization of Mass Media Firms* (New York: Priority Press Publications, 1991), pp. 24-26; for information on German expansion, see June Carolyn Erlick, "Time-Warner to Launch German Channel in '93," *Multichannel News*, April 13, 1992.

67. Reuven Frank, interview with author, February 6, 1992.

68. Eason Jordan, vice president for international news gathering, CNN, interview with author, Atlanta, August 12, 1992.

69. Thomas L. Friedman, "Clinton's Aides Search for Options and Offices, *New York Times*, November 16, 1992, p. A14.

70. Stuart H. Loory and Ann Imse, *Seven Days that Shook the World* (Atlanta: Turner Publishing, 1991), p. 235.

71. By his own account, Bessmertnykh refused to join the coup. But he issued ambiguous cables to Soviet diplomatic missions, calling for them to put a "good face" on the coup, and was fired by Gorbachev for having buttressed the authority of the coup leaders. See Woodward, *The Commanders*, p. 58; Loory and Imse, *Seven Days that Shook the World*, pp. 72-73.

72. Vesey, interview with author, May 27, 1992.

73. Timothy J. McNulty, "Decisions at the Speed of Satellite," *Chicago Tribune*, December 22, 1991, p. 1.

74. After the coup, ABC's Diane Sawyer scooped CNN with her interview of Boris Yeltsin, although CNN president Tom Johnson responded with shuttle diplomacy that brought Gorbachev on CNN's air.

75. Christopher Irwin, "Inaugural Lecture," Singapore Press Club, Singapore, September 27, 1991.

76. Eduard Shevardnadze, "The Tragedy of Gorbachev," *Newsweek*, September 9, 1991, pp. 30-31.

77. Daniel C. Hallin and Paolo Mancini, "The Summit as Media Event: The Reagan/Gorbachev Meetings on U.S., Italian, and Soviet Television," in Jay G. Blumler, Jack M. McLeod, and Karl Erik Rosengren, *Comparatively Speaking: Communication and Culture across Space and Time* (Newbury Park, Calif.: Sage, 1992).

78. I would like to thank my colleagues at the University of Wisconsin-Madison, School of Journalism and Mass Communication—James L. Baughman, Jo Ellen Fair, and Hemant Shah—for their careful and thoughtful comments on this paper. Carmen Sirianni of Brandeis, Andrea Walsh of Harvard, and David Merrill helped get it and keep it on track. CNN was very helpful at every stage of my research; I specially want to thank Alyssa Levy and Steve Haworth. Jill of the BBC World Service was also very helpful. Ralph Hurwitz literally got the project in the air, and Robert Horwitz of University of California-San Diego and Jon Cruz of University of California-Santa Barbara have been ongoing sources of important criticism and assistance. I also would like to thank my editor at the Twentieth Century Fund, Suzanne Charlé, for both her ongoing editorial advice and patience, as well as Michelle Miller and staff who offered comments. Finally, Stacey Oliker of University of Wisconsin-Milwaukee offered editorial advice when I most needed it, at every stage of this project.

Index

About the Author

Lewis A. Friedland is an assistant professor in the School of Journalism and Mass Communication at the University of Wisconsin-Madison, where he is an associate of the Mass Communication Research Center and the head of the Broadcast Sequence. Before coming to Madison, Friedland was executive producer at CBS affiliate WITI, Milwaukee. His work has won national and regional awards, including the Society of Professional Journalists Public Service Award in 1990. He remains an active producer and program consultant with Wisconsin Public Television.